Contents

About this Book

KEY TO SYMBOLS

⊞ map reference to the maps found in the What to See section (see below)

⊠ address or location

☎ telephone number

🕓 opening times

🍴 restaurant or café on premises or near by

🚇 Rouen Métrobus

🚌 nearest bus/tram route

🚃 nearest overground train station

⛴ ferry crossings and boat excursions

ℹ tourist information

♿ facilities for visitors with disabilities

✋ admission charge

↔ other places of interest near by

❓ other practical information

➤ indicates the page where you will find a fuller description

✈ travel by air

Essential Normandy is divided into five sections to cover the most important aspects of your visit to Normandy.

Viewing Normandy pages 5–14
An introduction to Normandy by the author
Normandy's Features
Essence of Normandy
The Shaping of Normandy
Peace and Quiet
Normandy's Famous

Top Ten pages 15–26
The author's choice of the Top Ten places to see in Normandy, listed in alphabetical order, each with practical information.

What to See pages 27–90
The three main areas of Normandy, each with its own brief introduction and an alphabetical listing of the main attractions
Practical information
Snippets of 'Did you know…' information
2 suggested walks
4 suggested tours
2 features

Where To... pages 91–116
Detailed listings of the best places to eat, stay, shop, take the children and be entertained.

Practical Matters pages 117–24
A highly visual section containing essential travel information.

Maps
All map references are to the individual maps found in the What to See section of this guide.
For example, Dieppe has the reference ⊞ 29E4 – indicating the page on which the map is located and the grid square in which the town is to be found. A list of the maps that have been used in this travel guide can be found in the index.

Prices
Where appropriate, an indication of the cost of an establishment is given by **£** signs:
£££ denotes higher prices, **££** denotes medium prices, while **£** denotes lower charges.

Star Ratings
Most of the places described in this book have been given a separate rating:

✪✪✪   Do not miss
✪✪   Highly recommended
✪   Worth seeing

Viewing
Normandy

Above and right: *two
Norman delights – apples on
the bough and music in the
streets*

5

Nia Williams's Normandy

Hearth and Home
Timber-framed houses and barns are found all over central and northeast Normandy. The frames, fitted together on the ground and hoisted into place, have either an infill of clay, straw and manure, or the added strength and decoration of brick. In central and west Normandy golden Caen stone gives town buildings a mellow glow, and on the sea-battered northwestern coast dark granite is used to withstand the elements.

Normandy is a region that denies any simple description. Its long coastline takes in family resorts, lonely windswept dunes and rocky cliffs, while inland there are marshlands, deep river gorges and gentle farmland. Indeed, the whole region is composed of natural 'territories', such as the Pays d'Auge, the Perche and the Suisse Normande.

Time often seems to have frozen in the villages and ancient woodlands – but my own fascination is with the history that survives in the Normandy landscape. To me, the crumbling abbey ruins tell a turbulent story of religious fervour, scholarly debate and revolutionary destruction. A solid donjon, an elegant château or a market town's startlingly elaborate parish church all speak of the changing fortunes of a once formidable political power. And I am equally drawn to the many towns that have recovered and reinvented themselves after wartime devastation; after all, the concrete and glass town that replaced Le Havre's shattered centre is as evocative in its way as are the bunkers and war museums of the D-Day beaches.

We each come in search of a different Normandy: some to see the salvaged architecture of Rouen's glorious past, or the bizarre, man-made peak of le Mont-St-Michel. Others come to remember the battles of 1944 – or simply to enjoy the delicious cider, calvados, cheese and seafood. Whatever you search for in your own Normandy, this large, varied and always surprising region is unlikely to disappoint.

Left: the 12th-century Château Gaillard still dominates the town of les Andelys

Normandy's Features

Geography

- 14,500km of rivers and streams. Longest river: the Seine.
- 600km of coastline.
- Highest hills: Mont des Avaloirs and the Signal d'Écouves (both 417m).
- Regional parks: Parc Naturel Régional de Brotonne (58,000ha); Parc Naturel Régional Normandie-Maine (234,000ha); Parc Naturel Régional des Marais du Cotentin et du Bessin (125,000ha).
- Regions: Haute-Normandie (upper Normandy) and Basse-Normandie (lower Normandy).
- Area: Haute-Normandie – 12,301sq km; Basse-Normandie – 17,589sq km.

Much of Normandy's landscape reflects the importance of dairy farming in its economy

Politics and Society

- Five *départements* (administrative areas): Seine-Maritime and Eure (Haute-Normandie); Manche, Orne and Calvados (Basse-Normandie).
- Population: Haute-Normandie – 1,760,000; Basse-Normandie – 1,404,000; Rouen – 380,100.
- Main regional newspaper: *Paris-Normandie*, produced at Rouen.
- Main religion: Roman Catholicism.

Transport and Industry

- Main economic activities: farming, fishing, tourism, textiles, oil refining.
- Major ferry ports: Cherbourg, Dieppe, Le Havre and Ouistreham.
- Main bridges across the Seine: Pont de Normandie (1995) – 2,141m long; Pont de Tancarville (1959) – 1,400m long; Pont de Brotonne (1977) – 1,280m long.

Say the Word

Norman place-names and family names are a mixture of Scandinavian, English and Frankish influences. The language once used by Normans has survived – just – as a patois spoken by a diminishing number on the Channel Islands. Linguists describe it as having a harder, more guttural sound than standard French, and it uses expressions derived from English and the Scandinavian languages.

Essence of Normandy

Normandy's greatest attraction is its variety, and each visit reveals new discoveries. The northeast coast offers old-fashioned seaside resorts, complete with mini-golf and fish stalls; the central Côte Fleurie is where up-market sun-worshippers display their jewellery; and in the west visitors can enjoy deserted dunes and wild rocky shores. Inland there are opportunities for hikers, canoeists and horse riders; and for lovers of architecture and history there's no shortage of medieval abbeys, beautiful churches, ruined castles and formidable châteaux. The only problem is deciding where the essence of Normandy lies for you.

THE 10 ESSENTIALS

*If you only have a short time to visit Normandy,
or would like to get a really complete picture of
the region, here are the essentials:*

• **Climb to the top** of le Mont-St-Michel (▶ 24–25) – it's a long haul, but well worth it for the outstanding views of the bay and the mount itself, casting its distinctive shadow across the sands.

• **Stroll through the beech woods** – the Forêt de Lyons, for example (▶ 43) – and enjoy their grace and silvery light.

• **Order a dish of fresh seafood** (*assiette de fruits de mer*) at a harbourside restaurant in Dieppe or Honfleur (▶ 21, 23).

• **Buy a snack** at a *pâtisserie*: there's one in nearly every town and village, and whatever you choose will be fresh and delicious.

• **Get off the beaten track** and explore the inland countryside: abbeys, châteaux and other sites are well signposted, and timber-framed farm buildings and turreted mansions can be found even along the most remote and unpromising country lanes.

• **Drive to the tip of the Cotentin peninsula (Cap de la Hague)** and look out past the lighthouse for dramatic views across the English Channel (▶ 82).

• **See the 'land of horses'** from horseback (▶ 115) – or watch the best of the breeds on parade at le Pin-au-Haras national stud (▶ 70).

• **Browse among the stalls** of one of the weekly markets (▶ 107), where you can find a rich assortment of fresh fruit and vegetables, live chickens and rabbits, home-baked cakes, antiques …

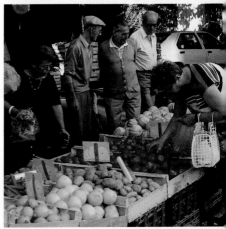

• **Cross the Seine** by ferry at Duclair, west of Rouen, or across the bow-backed Pont de Normandie, for a sense of the meandering course of the river.

• **Get a real taste of Normandy** by trying cider with your meal, a selection of the region's cheeses (▶ 76–77), and a *trou normand* – a glass of calvados between courses.

*Fermented apples are used to make the popular brandy, calvados
Above: fresh fruit and vegetables on sale in a Normandy market
Left: fishing boats unload their catch at the Dieppe quayside*

The Shaping of Normandy

900 BC
Celts arrive in northeast France and settle along the Seine (the 'tin road'), trading Cornish tin.

58–1 BC
Much of Normandy becomes part of Roman 'Armorica'. Walled towns are built – *Rotomagus* (Rouen), *Mediolanum* (Évreux), *Noviomagus* (Lisieux), *Caracotinum* (Harfleur).

3rd–5th centuries AD
Christianity begins to spread. Germanic migrations.

485–500
As the Roman Empire disintegrates the Franks, led by Clovis, occupy parts of Normandy.

6th–8th centuries
Religious centres founded at St-Wandrille (649), Jumièges (654), le Mont-St-Michel (709).

800
First coastal raids by Vikings ('Northmen').

9th century
Vikings make their way along the Seine, attacking Rouen and Jumièges (841), and reach Bayeux in 858.

911
King Charles the Simple accepts the Vikings' presence, making their leader Rollo (Hrølf the Walker) the first duke of Normandy.

933
Cotentin peninsula brought into the duchy by Duke William Longsword.

1027
Birth of William the Bastard (later the Conqueror) to Duke Robert of Normandy at Falaise.

1066
Norman invasion of England. Duke William defeats Harold at Hastings and becomes king of England.

1087
William dies in Rouen and is buried in the Abbaye aux Hommes, Caen.

1204
King John of England loses Normandy to Philippe Auguste, king of France.

1315
Norman charter gives the region independent tax-raising powers.

1346
Hundred Years War between France and England begins with the invasion of Normandy by King Edward III of England.

1431
Jeanne d'Arc, reviver of French fortunes, is burned at the stake in Rouen by the English.

1450
King Charles VII of France regains Normandy.

1517
New port established at Le Havre.

1589
After years of religious war, Protestant King Henri IV of France defeats Catholics at Arques and Ivry-la-Bataille. Edict of Nantes (1598) grants limited rights to Huguenots (Protestants).

1608
Samuel de Champlain leaves Honfleur to found Québec.

1685
Revocation of the Edict of Nantes by Louis XIV. Mass emigration of Huguenots leaves the Norman textile industry in decline.

1789
The French Revolution: Caen is a stronghold of the republican Girondin faction – but much of Normandy remains royalist.

1793
Girondins lay siege to Granville and defeat its Chouan (royalist) defenders.

1806–43
Development of coastal

Left: a triumphal statue of William the Conqueror in his birthplace, Falaise

resorts, helped by the growth of railways, and ships between Dieppe and Newhaven, England.

1883–1926
Impressionist painter Claude Monet lives and works at Giverny.

1940
German occupation of Normandy.

1944
D-Day landings by British, Commonwealth and American forces; the Battle of Normandy.

1954
Election of a new president of the Republic, René Coty, native of Le Havre.

1967
La Hague nuclear processing plant opens on Cotentin peninsula.

1974–5
Brotonne and Normandie-Maine regional parks are

American troops approach the Normandy coast on 6 June 1944

created to protect nature and heritage.

1980
Greenpeace ship *Rainbow Warrior* pursues a vessel carrying nuclear waste into Cherbourg harbour.

1983–4
Two nuclear power stations opened: Flamanville and Paluel.

1994
Fiftieth anniversary commemorations of D-Day.

2001
Work starts on the 2.2ha Juno Beach Museum and Information Centre, Courseulles-sur-Mer, Caen – a memorial to Canadian forces who landed on Juno Beach on D-Day. Due to open in June 2002.

Peace & Quiet

There are many ways to escape the crowds in this predominantly rural region, though few offer complete silence. Peace and quiet can mean the crashing waves on a wild coastline, or the birdsong and rustling leaves of an ancient beech forest. Only the cemeteries of World War II are places of truly profound silence.

The Countryside

The classic Norman landscape is one of scattered timber-framed farmhouses, grazing cattle, orchards and meadows. The apples and pears of the Pays d'Auge, a swathe of fertile rolling country around Lisieux, produce cider and the famous calvados brandy, while the the dairy farms provide exquisite cheeses. To the west, the area along the Orne river known as the Suisse Normande is more dramatic, its craggy slopes and wooded gorges ideal for walkers and climbers. Farther west again, at the base of the Cotentin peninsula, the region resumes a gentle, pastoral character in the *bocage*, where fields are separated by deep lanes and thick hedges. In the spring these hedgerows burst into colour as a mass of wild flowers comes into bloom.

The Forests

Normandy retains vast tracts of beech, oak and pine forest. The Forêt de Brotonne, a dense woodland enclosed in a loop of the Seine, forms the focus of the 58,000ha

The tranquil Forêt de Perseigne, a mixed wood of beech, oak and coniferous trees

Parc Naturel Régional de Brotonne. In the region's deep south the Parc Naturel Régional Normandie-Maine takes in several forests, including the 14,000ha Forêt d'Écouves, where deer and roebuck roam, and the Forêt de Perseigne (► 56) east of Alençon. The pretty village of Lyons-la-Forêt (► 43) is a perfect base for exploring the Forêt de Lyons, 11,000ha of soaring beech trees (*hêtres*). All these woodlands have rambling trails and waymarked paths.

The Cotentin (Cherbourg) Peninsula

The coastline along the northwest finger of this large peninsula takes on the stark, rugged beauty that characterises the neighbouring region of Brittany. The Cap de la Hague (► 82), at the farthest tip of land, is the place for windswept walks and wide views across the fast-flowing waters of the Alderney Race towards the Channel Islands. From here the road sweeps south to follow the western side of the peninsula past the Vauville dunes that shelter sea birds, butterflies and the tiny spring dwarf pansy. Quiet resorts such as Barneville-Carteret (► 81) punctuate long, empty beaches lower down the coast. The eastern Cotentin offers a softer landscape of woods and pastures, especially along the Val de Saire, inland of Barfleur and St-Vaast-la-Hougue.

The granite cliffs of the Cotentin peninsula, Normandy's wildest stretch of coastline

The War Cemeteries

Many people come to Normandy specifically to pay tribute to the dead of World War II; others visit the cemeteries for solitude and reflection (► 71). Among the largest British cemeteries are Bayeux, Ranville (near Pegasus Bridge), Tilly-sur-Seulles (between Caen and Balleroy) and Ryes (northeast of Bayeux). American cemeteries are found at St-James (between Avranches and Fougères) and Colleville-sur-Mer, while the main German cemetery is at la Cambe, northeast of Isigny-sur-Mer.

The legacy of war. Ranks of British gravestones at Ranville

Normandy's Famous

Best of the Rest

Among other people of letters and the arts associated with Normandy are: composer Erik Satie (1866–1925), born in Honfleur; painters Jean-François Millet (1814–75), born near Cherbourg, and Fernand Léger (1881–1955), from Argentan; political philosopher Alexis de Tocqueville (1805–59), whose ancestral château is on the Cotentin peninsula; Rouen-born dramatist Pierre Corneille (1606–84); writer Guy de Maupassant (1850–93), born near Dieppe; and novelist Marcel Proust (1871–1922), who often spent his holidays in Cabourg.

A self-portrait by Claude Monet (1917), painted during his years at Giverny

William the Conqueror

The future conqueror of England (1027–87) was born in Falaise (▶ 65), the illegitimate son of Robert the Magnificent, Duke of Normandy. After inheriting the duchy at the age of eight, he spent later years fighting hostile relatives, Norman rebels and the king of France. In return for his help during King Edward the Confessor's exile William was allegedly promised the English throne; when Edward died in 1066 he set off with an invasion fleet to claim it, defeating his rival, King Harold, at Battle near Hastings. Reputedly strong and cruel, William was also a clever politician and a devoted husband.

Gustave Flaubert

Flaubert (1821–80) grew up at the Hôtel-Dieu in Rouen where his father was a physician (▶ 33). His first novel, *Madame Bovary* (1857), caused a sensation with its account of the affairs and eventual suicide of a bored, young doctor's wife. Flaubert, along with his publisher and printer, was taken to court but cleared of offending public morals. His next work, *Salammbô* (1862), depicted the brutality and exoticism of ancient Carthage, and in *L'Éducation sentimentale* (1869) he described the lives and loves of mid-19th-century Parisians.

Claude Monet

Born in Paris, Monet (1840–1926) went to school in Le Havre where, at the age of 18, he met picture-framer-turned-artist Eugène Boudin (▶ 22, 23). Under Boudin's influence Monet abandoned the studio to paint directly from nature, using the colour and light of the Norman coast to full effect. His *Impression: Soleil levant* (1872) provided the famous label for a contemporary group of painters who strove for atmosphere rather than realism in their work. After years of poverty Monet found success in the 1880s and moved to Giverny where he created a beautiful garden, the subject of many paintings (▶ 42). He experimented with light and colour, producing a series of studies of Rouen cathedral in the 1890s that showed the changing effects of sunlight.

Top Ten

Above: *colourful fishing
boats at Honfleur*
Right: *William the Conqueror
on campaign*

1
Abbaye de Jumièges

✚ 38B1

✉ 27km west of Rouen, on D143

Once a centre of scholarship and worship, this magnificent abbey was plundered after the French Revolution and is now a haunting ruin.

With its soaring white towers, circled by rooks, Jumièges has a strangely unsettling effect. The earliest ruins – the Église St-Pierre – date from the 10th century when the Benedictine abbey was refounded to replace the 7th-century original burned by Vikings. In 1040 work began on a second church, Notre-Dame, conse-crated in the presence of Duke William the Bastard. During the following 300 years Jumièges prospered, accumulating gifts and adding new buildings.

With the Hundred Years War Jumièges entered a period of insecurity and slow decline; by 1792 there were only seven resident monks and the abbey was closed. It then passed to a series of private owners: one tried to set up a factory in it; another blew up the chancel and sold off the stone. Only in 1824 did new owners put a halt to the destruction.

Notre-Dame is the most spectacular part of the former monastic complex. Its twin western towers – once with timber spires – flank the entrance into a vast roofless nave lined with bold arcades. Beyond the transepts, where the northwest column has an intricate carving of a bird, a delicate 13th-century lancet arch marks the site of the chancel chapels. 'Charles VII's Passageway' leads to the Église St-Pierre, whose own towers have now gone except for their rectangular bases. Only the outline remains of the cloisters. Behind the abbey, a flight of curving steps leads up to the 17th-century abbot's lodgings, still intact, and a small knot-garden.

☎ 02 35 37 24 02

🕐 Apr to mid-Jun, mid-Sep to Oct, daily 9–12, 2–5 (weekend 6); mid-Jun to mid-Sep daily 9–6:30; Nov–Mar, daily 10–12, 2–6 (weekend 5). Closed 1 Jan, 1 May, 1 Nov, 11 Nov, 25 Dec

🍴 Auberge des Ruines (££), place de la Mairie

🚌 30 from Rouen (change buses at Duclair)

✋ Expensive

↔ Rouen (▶ 26, 31–36)

Above: the abbey's towers seen from the south

2

Les Andelys & Château Gaillard

A historic timber-framed village lies at the foot of the hill where Richard the Lionheart's castle has panoramic views over the Seine Valley.

Situated on the edge of a deep loop in the Seine, at the northern end of the Forêt des Andelys, are the two towns of les Andelys. Petit Andely grew in the shadow of King Richard's castle while Grand Andely is a busy centre with a Saturday market. The ruins of **Château Gaillard** rise from a high chalk outcrop; from a distance they are barely distinguishable from the white cliffs. Richard had the castle hastily constructed – probably between 1196 and 1198 – though it became known as his 'one-year wonder' because of the speed in which it was built.

One of the five original towers still stands, as well as part of the donjon, the later governor's lodge and the curtain walls. While these squat remains still preserve an impenetrable appearance, the château fell to the French just six years after its completion, when King Philippe Auguste's soldiers entered through the latrines.

Below Château Gaillard, Petit Andely extends along the riverside, a fine collection of stone and timber buildings with carved lintels, coloured glass and swirling iron lampholders. Galleries and restaurants line the street, leading into a peaceful cobbled square overlooked by the Église St-Sauveur. Grand Andely itself has some fine town houses, as well as the 13th- to 17th-century Église Notre-Dame. The Musée Nicolas Poussin houses paintings by the artist, and the Musée Normandie-Niémen commemorates General de Gaulle's fighter squadron.

🕂 29E3

🍴 Choice of restaurants (£–£££)

🚌 From Évreux, marked 'les Andelys'

Château Gaillard

☎ 02 32 54 04 16

🕐 Mid-Mar to mid-Nov, Wed afternoon–Mon 9–12, 2–6

♿ None

↔ Écouis (► 38)

✋ Cheap

Massive walls and a broad view of the Seine were the strengths of Château Gaillard

3
Bayeux: the Tapestry

✚ 50B5

✉ Centre Guillaume le
Conquérant, rue de
Nesmond

☎ 02 31 51 25 50

🕐 May–Aug and Easter
weekend, 9–7; mid-Mar
to Apr and Sep–Oct,
9–6:30; Nov to mid-Mar,
9:30–12:30, 2–6. Closed
1, 2 Jan, 25–6 Dec

🍴 Choice of restaurants
and cafés in town
(£–££)

♿ Good

✋ Moderate

*All the colour, character and action of a good
film are captured in this 70m-long tapestry,
commissioned to celebrate William the Conqueror's
victory at Hastings.*

William's half-brother Odo, Bishop of Bayeux, decided to
decorate his new cathedral with a spectacular wall-hanging
– the latest thing in religious fashion – to impress pilgrims
and local people coming to the church. A team of embroi-
derers took several years to complete the frieze in eight
different-coloured wools (blues, greens, reds and mustard
yellow). The result, now displayed in a former seminary,
traces the Norman dispute over the English royal inheri-
tance. It begins with the aged King Edward sending his
brother-in-law Earl Harold Godwinson to Normandy to
inform William (allegedly) he will be the next English king.
Harold's adventures include shipwreck, capture and
rescue, and a thrilling ride with William's troops against the
duke of Brittany.

*Duke William and Earl
Harold in discussion at
the palace of Rouen*

Before seeing the tapestry, visitors are led past a long
but useful exhibition, which suggests that the tapestry
deliberately includes flashbacks and split-screen effects for
dramatic impact. An audio-visual commentary then guides
you all too quickly past the genuine article. The wealth of
detail deserves a much longer browse: spies listening to
royal conversations; the Saxons sporting droopy
moustaches; Halley's Comet shooting ominously over
Harold's coronation; food and wine being loaded for the
invasion fleet; and, in the final battle scenes, horses
mustering, galloping and falling while, in the tapestry
margins, soldiers' corpses are stripped of their armour. It's
so fresh and energetic that you can almost hear the din of
a battle fought over 900 years ago.

4
Caen: le Mémorial

Outstanding among Normandy's many war museums, this 'Museum for Peace' examines the events leading up to World War II and looks into an uncertain future.

Across the limestone façade of le Mémorial runs the inscription: *'La douleur m'a brisée, la fraternité m'a relevée ... de ma blessure a jailli un fleuve de liberté'* ('Grief crushed me, fraternity revived me ... from my wound there sprang a river of freedom'). Conflict and hope are the themes of this museum. Hovering over the vast entrance hall is a British Hawker Typhoon aircraft; a caption notes that its 23-year-old pilot was killed when it was shot down in 1944. This is not a museum of military hardware or cold strategy: throughout its themed 'spaces' individual experience is set against the progress of world affairs. Spaces One to Three trace events from 1918 to 1944 along a spiralling walkway that descends into near-darkness. Archive material includes letters, film, photographs and a secretly taped phone conversation between the collaborator Weygand and his delegate to the armistice talks. There are harrowing images: the hopeless faces of concentration camp victims; a 17-year-old Russian patriot about to be hanged.

Beyond the walkway, displays include personal letters and footage of hand-to-hand fighting during the German advance on Stalingrad. In spaces Four and Five documentary and fictional film recreates the 1944 invasion. Post-war conflict and diplomacy are covered in Jacques Perrin's film *Hope* in Space Six, and the final space is a gallery devoted to winners of the Nobel Peace Prize.

✚ 50C4

✉ esplanade du Général Eisenhower

☎ 02 31 06 06 44

🕐 Jul–Aug, 9–8; Sep–Jun, 9–7. Closed 1–15 Jan, last Sun in Jan, 25 Dec. Last entry 75 mins before closing

🍴 Restaurant and café (££)

🚌 17 from Tour le Roy in Caen centre

♿ Very good

✋ Expensive

A Typhoon aircraft hangs above pictures of the casualties of war in le Mémorial's foyer

5
Château d'O

Mirrored in the waters of its moat, the towers and pointed roofs of Château d'O give it a fairy-tale charm.

 51D2

☎ 02 33 35 34 69

🕐 Apr–Oct, 2:30–6; Nov–Mar, 2:30–5. Closed Tue except Jul and Aug, also 1 Jan, 25 Dec

🍴 La Ferme du Château d'O (££–£££) ☎ 02 33 35 36 87

🚌 12 from Alençon to Mortrée

♿ None

✋ Expensive

↔ Argentan (► 55), Château de Sassy (► 73), Sées (► 74)

This romantic château was built in 1484 for Jean d'O, Charles VIII's chamberlain, on the foundations of an 11th-century fortress. In 1590 a western wing was added by Jean's powerful descendant, François d'O. Having risen from governor of Caen to Henri III's superintendent of finance, François manoeuvred his way through the controversy and changing alliances of the Religious Wars, and emerged as Henri IV's counsellor. During his career he was accused of pocketing royal funds for his own use – partly to spend on this family seat.

Elaborate carvings decorate the oldest part of the château, the gatehouse, while an arcade and windows with decorative iron grilles line the 16th-century south wing. Red and black brick patterns occasionally break the pale gold and grey stone of the façade, and the O family emblem, the ermine, is carved on the south wing. A walkway leads across the moat into a three-sided courtyard, with further intricate carvings decorating the walls. Inside, the furnishings date mainly from the 18th century, and include *trompe l'œils* of Apollo and the Nine Muses, and eagles in flight, uncovered in the west wing during renovation work. The château grounds are as tranquil as the building itself: a path leads through the simple garden to woodland, and past the chapel to the orangery where exhibitions are occasionally held. Beyond the south wing, the farm buildings that once housed some of the château's household are now a restaurant.

The château's courtyard and towers, reflected in its moat

6
Dieppe

This energetic, modern harbour town, with its delightful old quarters, offers visitors arriving by ferry a compelling first taste of France.

There's something irresistibly cheerful about Dieppe, even though it could do with a coat of paint. Once cross-Channel ferries deposited passengers opposite the quai Henri IV's hotels and restaurants, where they could then tuck into fresh seafood while watching the latest catch being unloaded on to quayside stalls. Now the ferry terminal has been shifted out of sight, yachts have moved in, and the fish stalls have been moved aside to make way for a car park. But there is still a lively pulse to the town, especially in the pedestrianised centre.

Across the water from the end of quai Henri IV the clifftop Église Notre-Dame de Bon-Secours watches over the port. The road then swings round to the shingle beach where grand old houses line the boulevard de Verdun and, in summer, snack stalls are set out along the boulevard du Maréchal Foch that runs parallel. Looming over all at the west end of the town is the 15th-century castle, whose **Musée du Château** houses a collection of carved ivory – a speciality of Dieppe in the 17th century – and paintings by Renoir, Boudin, Pissarro and Braque.

Narrow alleys lined with crumbling old houses lead from the promenade and quayside into the centre of town and to the 14th- to 16th-century Église St-Jacques, its fabric slowly being eaten away by the elements. Inside is a frieze of Brazilian natives rescued from the palace of Jean Ango, François I's naval adviser, whose fleet of priva-teers captured more than 300 Portuguese ships in the 16th century. Northeast, in the old fishing quarter, the **Cité de la Mer** has exhibi-tions on shipbuilding, sea life and geology.

The Grande Rue in Dieppe, always full of colour and bustle

✚ 29E4

🍴 Choice of seafood restaurants on quai Henri IV (£–££)

🚌 15B from Rouen

↔ Arques-la-Bataille (► 37), Château de Miromesnil (► 43), Varengeville (► 47)

Musée du Château

✉ rue Chastes

☎ 02 35 84 19 76

🕐 Jun–Sep, daily 10–12, 2–6; Oct–May, Wed–Mon 10–12, 2–5 (Sun 6). Closed 1 Jan, 1 May, 1 Nov, 25 Dec

♿ Few

✋ Cheap

Cité de la Mer

✉ rue de l'Asile Thomas

☎ 02 35 06 93 20

🕐 Sep–Apr, daily 10–12, 2–6; May–Aug, 10–7. Closed 25 Dec–2 Jan

♿ Good

✋ Moderate

7
Le Havre: Musée des Beaux-Arts André Malraux

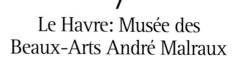

✚ 38A1

✉ 2 boulevard Clémenceau

☎ 02 35 19 62 62

🕐 Mon, Wed, Thu, Fri
11–6; Sat, Sun 11–7

🍴 Café (££)

♿ Very good

✋ Cheap

🔁 Honfleur (▶ 23)

This striking modern building, with its highly original walls of glass, houses an excellent display of French paintings.

Le Havre can be an oppressive place, with its endless apartment blocks and the concrete centre erected quickly after the devastation of the old town by air raids in 1944 (▶ 42). For anyone interested in Normandy's artistic heritage, though, it has the best gallery in the region.

Named after the novelist and art critic André Malraux (1901–76), the museum has undergone extensive renovation, making the most of its view over the port (through a large concrete sculpture nicknamed 'The Eye') and removing partitions inside to allow even greater light and space.

Music at the Customs House at Le Havre *by Raoul Dufy*

Malraux devised the concept of 'the museum without walls', and this building comes as near as possible to fulfilling that idea. One feature is that visitors can choose how to view the paintings: chronologically from the 17th to the 20th centuries, or beginning with the famous collection of works by Eugène Boudin (1824–98) and Raoul Dufy (1877–1953).

Boudin, who was born near by in Honfleur, represents French Impressionism along with Monet, Renoir and others. His love of painting out in the open, using free brushwork to convey the coast's huge skies and seas, earned him the title 'painter of beaches' and provided inspiration for Monet. Dufy was a native of Le Havre and one of the group of fauvist ('wild beast') painters who used bold colours to depict everyday scenes. Other artists featured include Corot, Manet, Millet and Courbet, and 17th- to 19th-century Dutch, Flemish and Italian painters.

8
Honfleur

This is one of the prettiest and most popular harbour towns in Normandy, with an old-world ambience and a distinguished maritime history.

Honfleur is about as attractive as a working port can be. Tall grey houses stand shoulder-to-shoulder along the Vieux Bassin (Old Dock), the focus of town, fishing boats cluster along the harbour near by, and shops, galleries, restaurants and hotels fill the many timber-framed and slate-fronted buildings.

The port has a long history. Its heyday as a seafaring centre was in the 17th century, when Samuel de Champlain set sail to found Québec; his achievement is noted on a plaque on the wall of the 16th-century Lieutenance, a ramshackle stone building guarding the harbour entrance, and once the home of the king's lieutenant, the governor of Honfleur. Église Ste-Catherine in the market place is remarkable for its construction by shipbuilders using wooden struts and tiles for both the main body and the 18m bell tower that stands alone across the square. The 15th-century church is dark but airy, like a great barn: two parallel naves are divided by slender timber columns and the vaulted ceiling has the look of an upturned boat. The second nave was added in 1496 to accommodate the prosperous town's growing population of sailors and ship-owners.

Not surprisingly, Honfleur was a magnet to artists in the 19th and 20th centuries. The **Musée Eugène Boudin**, named after the town's most famous son, has works by Dufy, Corot, Monet and the man himself.

✚ 38A1

🍴 Choice of restaurants and cafés (£–£££)

🚌 24 from Évreux; 28, 34 from Le Havre

↔ Le Havre (➤ 22, 42)

Musée Eugène Boudin

✉ rue de l'Homme-de-Bois, place Erik-Satie

☎ 02 31 89 54 00

🕐 Mid-Mar to Sep, Wed–Mon 10–12, 2–6; Oct–Mar, Wed–Mon 2:30–5, weekend 10–12, 2:30–5. Closed 1 Jan–10 Feb

♿ Few

✋ Moderate

Fishing boats moored in the Vieux Bassin, overlooked by distinctive, narrow dockside buildings

9
Le Mont-St-Michel

80B1

Choice of restaurants and cafés (£–£££)

29 from Granville; 30 from Pontorson

Few; no wheelchair access to upper Mont

Avranches (▶ 81)

Abbaye

☎ 02 33 89 80 00

🕐 May–Sep, daily 9–5:30; Oct–Apr, 9:30–4:30 (school hols 9:30–5)

✋ Expensive

Across its broad bay, le Mont-St-Michel rises like a vision, tapering up to the abbey spire from a chaotic pyramid of houses and shops.

In the early 8th century Bishop Aubert of Avranches had a vision in which the Archangel Michael ordered him to build a sanctuary on the isolated granite rock then known as Mont Tombe. This was no mean feat: apart from the problem of building on a sheer, narrow rock, the island is isolated by quicksands at low tide and deep water at high tide. Nevertheless, Aubert's church was finished in 708, and in the 10th century a monastery was founded on the site.

Over the centuries new buildings were added to the abbey and a town grew beneath it, clinging precariously to the steep sides. Buttresses and massive walls clamp everything fast to the rock, the church towering above the sands that have claimed the lives of many pilgrims on the last leg of their journey. Now the Mont is approached across a causeway and through the Porte du Roi. The winding Grande Rue, lined with souvenir shops and cafés, climbs towards the abbey, and steps lead off through narrow passages to the outer ramparts.

Finally, all routes lead to the **Abbaye** itself and the buildings known as 'la Merveille'. A trail passes through the refectory, cloisters and Knights' Hall, and past a huge wooden treadmill once operated by inmates when the abbey became a prison in the 18th century; the wheel was used to haul supplies straight up a

Right, top: *the Grande Rue, once crowded with medieval pilgrims, now with tourists*
Right: *le Mont, glorious in the early evening light*

steep ramp. Eventually steps lead down into the crypt where 10 massive columns support the abbey church. Outside, a tiny herb garden squeezed among turrets and chimneys looks out across the bay.

There are several museums on the Mont, as well as the Logis Tiphaine, home of the 14th-century military commander Bertrand du Guesclin.

10
Rouen: rue du Gros-Horloge

34B2

Choice of restaurants and cafés, especially in and around place du Vieux-Marché (£–£££)

15B from Dieppe

From Le Havre, Dieppe

Rouen (➤ 31–36), Jumièges (➤ 16), Martainville (➤ 43)

Tour du Beffroi

02 35 71 28 40

Apr to mid-Oct, Wed–Mon 10–1, 2–6. Closed 1, 8 May, 14 Jul, 15 Aug

Palais de Justice

8

None

Cheap

Ticket (panel, ➤ 33)

At the heart of Rouen's old town, this street is both a lively shopping centre and a showpiece of restored historic buildings.

There is much to admire along this pedestrianised route, where timber-framed houses have been smartly repaired, their woodwork painted in reds, pale orange and greens. The Gros-Horloge itself is an elaborate one-handed clock that sits on a stone archway spanning the street. It was originally set in the **Tour du Beffroi** (Belfry Tower) next door, but the citizens complained it was too difficult to see; so in 1527 the arch was purpose-built and the clock moved. Despite its single hand, the Gros-Horloge manages to tell time in hours, weeks and phases of the moon. The arch is covered in baroque carvings, including Christ the Shepherd and his flock.

The rue du Gros-Horloge links the two main focal points of old Rouen. At the west end is the place du Vieux-Marché where Jeanne d'Arc (Joan of Arc) was burned at the stake in 1431. The Église Ste-Jeanne d'Arc that marks the spot is one of Rouen's most evocative modern buildings: its wildly twisted cone of a roof extends to cover part of the central market in a design said to represent the flames that ended Joan's life. At the other end of the street is the cathedral square, dominated by the cathedral itself and surrounded by fine buildings including the city's oldest surviving Renaissance house, now the tourist office.

The Gros-Horloge, displayed for all to see on its 16th-century arch

26

What
to See

Above: *the intricate stonework of Rouen's cathedral*
Right: *delicate finery on show in the Alençon lace museum*

NORMANDY

0   20   40   60   80 km

GBA
Goury
Cap de la Hague
Nez de Jobourg
Cherbourg
Flamanville
Barfleur
Pointe de Barfleur
St-Vaast-la-Hougue
Valognes
Utah Beach
Ste-Mère-Eglise
Omaha Beach
Port-en-Bessin
Arromanches-les-Bains
Baie de la Seine
Houlgate
Cabourg
Barneville-Carteret
Cap de Carteret
Carentan
Isigny-sur-Mer
Bayeux
Château de Fontaine Henry
Ouistreham
GBJ
Lessay
Abbaye Cérisy-la-Forêt
St-Lô
Balleroy
Villers-Bocage
Caen
Coutances
Vire
Suisse Normande
Clécy
Falaise
Abbaye de Hambye
Villedieu-les-Poèles
Condé-sur-Noireau
Golfe de St-Malo
Granville
Abbaye de la Lucerne
Avranches
Vire
Flers
Argentan
St-Malo
Dinard
Cancale
le Mont-St-Michel
Sourdeval
Mortain
Domfront
Château de Sassy
la Ferté-Macé
Dol-de-Bretagne
Pontorson
St-Hilaire-du-Harcouët
Carrouges
Dinan
Antrain
Louvigné-du-Désert
Combourg
Rance
les Iffs
Fougères
Ernée
Mayenne
St-Léonard-des-Bois
St-Méen-le-Grand
Montfort
Liffré
Rennes
Vitré
Mayenne
Evron
Sillé-le-Guillaume
Mauron
Châteaugiron
Laval
Guer
Janzé
Retiers

28

Côte d'Albâtre

St-Valéry-sur-Somme

Abbeville

le Tréport • Eu

Dieppe

Blangy-sur-Bresle

Somme

Amiens

St-Valéry-en-Caux

Château de Miromesnil

Fécamp • Cany-Barville

Aumale

Cap d'Antifer

Etretat

Château de Galleville

Neufchâtel-en-Bray

Breteuil-sur-Noye

Château de Filières

Yvetot

Bolbec

Crèvecoeur-le-Grand

Montivilliers

Caudebec-en-Caux

Clères

Forges-les-Eaux

Harfleur

Lillebonne

Barentin

LE HAVRE

Pont de Normandie

Château d'Etelan

Rouen

Gournay-en-Bray

Honfleur

Abbaye de Jumièges

Seine

Lyons-la-Forêt

Beauvais

Trouville-sur-Mer

Pont-Audemer

Abbaye de Mortemer

Clermont

Deauville

le Bec-Hellouin

Ecouis

Thérain

Méru

Pont-l'Evêque

Château du Champ de Bataille

les Andelys

Gisors

Lisieux

Magny-en-Vexin

Pontoise

Crèvecoeur-en-Auge

St-Germain-de-Livet

le Neubourg

Château Gaillard

l'Isle-Adam

Livarot

Bernay

Vernon

Giverny

St-Denis

Vimoutiers

Evreux

Seine

St-Germain-en-Laye

Carnembert

Conches-en-Ouche

Mantes-la-Jolie

PARIS

Gacé

Breteuil

Anet

Versailles

l'Aigle

Houdan

Château d'O

Verneuil-sur-Avre

Dreux

Eure

Rambouillet

Sées

Senonches

Arpajon

Forêt d'Ecouves

Nogent-le-Roi

Epernon

Dourdan

Sarthe

Mortagne-au-Perche

la Loupe

Ablis

Etampes

Alençon

Bellême

Chartres

Mamers

Nogent-le-Rotrou

Illiers-Combray

Angerville

Bonnétable

la Ferté-Bernard

Loir

Bonneval

Toury

Brou

Pithiviers

Châteaudun

le Mans

Mondoubleau

Arnage

Circuit automobile

D

E

F

Left: *evening sun over the spires and bridges of Rouen*

Far left: 'Bienvenue en Normandie ...'

Rouen &
the Northeast

Northeast Normandy stands apart from the rest of the region. This is a flat windswept country that rises to a border of white cliffs along the Côte d'Albâtre (Alabaster Coast) and the Seine Valley. Resorts and harbour towns with long seafaring histories line the seaboard – Dieppe, Le Havre, Honfleur. Inland, the Pays de Caux plateau of Seine-Maritime is dotted with aged farmhouses, churches and châteaux, while ancient beech woods gather alongside the Seine.

Farther up the river, taking in part of the Eure *département*, lies the Normandie-Vexin, a historic administrative area once bitterly fought over by the medieval kings of England and France, and guarded by strongholds such as the mighty Château Gaillard (► 17). There is plenty to explore here, but no trip to upper Normandy is complete without a visit to its beautiful old capital, Rouen.

' Rouen, Geneva and Pisa have been tutresses of all I know, and were mistresses of all I did, from the first moments I entered their gates. '

John Ruskin
Praeterita
(1885–9)

Rouen

Old and new Rouen oppose each other across the Seine: the new suburbs on the south bank, with their offices and tower blocks, and on the north bank a forest of Gothic spires. Venture into the old town and you encounter a fascinating world of medieval streets and busy alleyways overshadowed by the jettied gables of timber-framed houses and shops (➤ 26).

Celts and Romans had settlements here, and a church stood on the cathedral site by AD 393. When Rollo led his Viking invaders into Normandy he chose Rouen for his capital, and by the 12th century it was being noted by a contemporary historian as a rich and pleasant town with 'great buildings, houses and churches'. A thriving weaving and textiles trade paid for more handsome buildings during the city's golden age, between the 15th and 17th centuries. After the disastrous bombardment of World War II many were painstakingly rebuilt, and today around 700 timber-framed houses survive.

But Rouen is not a city with a uniform heritage. Some streets were spared the bombing and still have a shabby, precarious look, particularly along rue St-Vivien; there you will find unpolished, lived-in corners that have changed little over the centuries. There are also striking examples of later architecture, such as the railway station. Rouen has managed to retain its character without a stifling reverence; its fine churches, museums, historic buildings and many architectural surprises are all part of a vibrant, modern city, with one of the most attractive centres in France.

Looking along the pretty rue Damiette towards the abbey church of St-Ouen

What to See in Rouen

🇫 34B2
✉ place de la Cathédrale
☎ 02 35 89 73 78
🕐 Daily. Guided tours:
Easter–early Sep,
Mon–Sat 10, 11, 2, 3, 4,
5, Sun 2, 3, 4, 5; early
Sep–Easter, Sat and Sun
between 10 and 6
🍴 Palais de Justice
🚌 3, 13
♿ None
💵 Tours moderate
↔ Rue du Gros-Horloge
(► 26),
Église St-Maclou (► 34)

CATHÉDRALE NOTRE-DAME   ✪✪✪

The process of cleaning and restoring the cathedral has long obscured its intricate west façade. But gradually it is emerging from the cocoon of scaffolding, revealing its delicately worked, glittering white stone, free from the patina of years of city life.

A cathedral has stood on this site since the 4th century, though the earliest parts of the present building – apart from some 11th-century fragments – are 13th-century. Two very different towers flank the façade, giving it an eccentric yet attractive appeal. The Tour St-Romain, on the left as you face the cathedral, is crowned with a steep slate roof decorated with gold sunbursts. On the right is the ornate Tour de Beurre (Butter Tower), a 16th-century addition apparently funded by the sale of dispensations to Rouen's rich, allowing them to enjoy butter and milk during Lent. The 151m central lantern tower, L'Aigle, with its cast-iron spire, was erected in 1876, replacing a 16th-century predecessor that had burned down.

Inside, beyond the soaring nave with its two-tiered arcades, the north transept contains a glorious 14th-century rose window and, rising from the balcony, the Escalier de la Librairie (Booksellers' Stairs). Traces of Roman columns can still be seen in the crypt, and effigies of Rollo, his son William Longsword, Henry, son of Henry II of England, and Richard the Lionheart are displayed in the ambulatory. The 14th-century Lady Chapel has two impressive tombs: one to the cardinals of Amboise, both called Georges, who are shown on their knees dressed in rich robes and framed by a Renaissance frieze; the other to Louis de Brézé whose wife, Diane de Poitiers, mistress of Henri II (► 37), is shown grieving over her husband.

Above: *the cardinals of Amboise, carved by Roulland le Roux on their 16th-century tomb*

32

MUSÉE DES ANTIQUITÉS ✪

Housed in a 17th-century convent, this extensive collection includes Egyptian, Greek, Gallo-Roman and medieval artefacts, including its star exhibit the famous 4th-century Mosaic of Lillebonne, the largest in France. Tapestries, tiles, Renaissance furniture and carved Rouennais façades are also on display. The natural history and ethnography museum is next door.

🔲 35C3
✉ 198 rue Beauvoisine
☎ 02 35 98 55 10
🕐 Mon–Sat 10–12:15, 1:30–5:30, Sun 2–6
🚌 Beauvoisine
♿ Few
💷 Cheap

MUSÉE DES BEAUX-ARTS ✪✪

Paintings by Velázquez, Fragonard, Géricault, Caravaggio, David, Renoir and Monet are on view in this grand civic building that overlooks a small park and ornamental pond. The collection, spanning five centuries, takes in Russian icons, Impressionism and Raymond Duchamp-Villon's vigorous modern sculpture.

🔲 34B2
✉ square Verdrel
☎ 02 35 71 28 40
🕐 Daily 10–6
🚌 Beaux-Arts
💷 Moderate
❓ Ticket (panel, ➤ below)

MUSÉE DE LA CÉRAMIQUE ✪

In the 17th and 18th centuries Rouen acquired fame and fortune producing faience, a style of tin-glazed earthenware with blue decoration on a white background or vice versa. Examples of this and other ceramics, including tableware and ornaments, are displayed in the 17th-century Hôtel d'Hocqueville, illustrating the industry's history.

🔲 34B2
✉ 1 rue Faucon
☎ 02 35 07 31 74
🕐 Daily 10–1, 2–6
🚌 Jeanne d'Arc
🚌 1, 2, 3, 4, 11, 13, 20, 22
♿ None
💷 Cheap
❓ Ticket (panel, ➤ below)

Ornate 18th-century faience in the Musée de la Céramique

> ### Did you know ?
>
> *A combined ticket allows admission to Tour du Beffroi (➤ 26), Musée des Beaux-Arts, Musée de la Céramique and Musée le Secq des Tournelles (➤ 34).*

MUSÉE FLAUBERT ET D'HISTOIRE DE LA MÉDECINE ✪

This dual-purpose museum in the 18th-century Hôtel-Dieu has memorabilia of Gustave Flaubert in the room where he was born (his father was a surgeon here), and miscellaneous tools used in 19th-century hospitals. Exhibits include a childbirth demonstrator, surgical instruments and, for times when all else failed, statues of healing saints.

🔲 34A2
✉ 51 rue de Lecat
☎ 02 35 15 59 95
🕐 Tue10–6, Wed–Sat 10–12, 2–6
🚌 Flaubert
♿ Few
💷 Free

33

An alfresco lunch on rue Damiette, between the churches of St-Maclou and St-Ouen

---

🚩 34B2

✉ 2 rue Jacques Villon

☎ 02 35 71 28 40

🕐 Wed 2–6, Thu–Mon 10–12, 2–6

🍴 Beaux-Arts

🚌 1, 2, 3, 4, 11, 13, 20, 22

💰 Cheap

❓ Ticket (panel, ➤ 33)

🚩 34B2

✉ rue aux Juifs

☎ 02 35 88 55 88

🕐 Wed 2–6, Thu–Mon 10–6

🍴 Palais de Justice

🚌 8, 2, 28

💰 Free

↔ rue du Gros-Horloge (➤ 26)

🚩 35C1

✉ place Barthélemy

MUSÉE LE SECQ DES TOURNELLES ●●

The 15th-century Église St-Laurent, all flying buttresses and tracery, is an apt setting for one of Rouen's most intriguing museums. On display is a collection of wrought ironwork in every imaginable form, from an elegant 18th-century banister (taken from the Château de Bellevue) to the loops and swirls of old shop signs, keys, door knockers and painful-looking corsets.

PALAIS DE JUSTICE ●●

When Normandy was granted its own *parlement* in 1514 the city's new exchequer building and merchants' hall was chosen to house the debating chamber and law court. It certainly provided due pomp and decoration: pinnacles, gargoyles, statuettes and tracery cluster about the steep-pitched, grey roofs in a Gothic frenzy. Excavations in the palace courtyard uncovered the Monument Juif (Jewish Monument), the remains of a late-11th-century synagogue.

RUE DU GROS-HORLOGE (➤ 26, TOP TEN)

ST-MACLOU, ÉGLISE ●●●

Badly damaged during World War II, this extravagant Flamboyant church finally reopened in 1980 after years of careful restoration. It was built between 1437 and 1517,

The 20m Croix de la Réhabilitation marks the scene of Joan of Arc's death (place du Vieux-Marché)

☎ 02 32 08 32 40 (Syndicat Initiative)
🕐 Mon–Sat, 10–12, 2–5:30; Sun 3–5:30
🚇 Palais de Justice
🚌 13, 3
💷 Free
↔ Gros-Horloge (▶ 26), Cathédrale Notre-Dame (▶ 32)

dedicated to St Malo, a 7th-century missionary possibly of Welsh origin. Its wooden doors and stone porch are overwhelmed with carvings, some dating back to the 1550s, others decapitated deliberately. To the left of the porch a Renaissance fountain shows Bacchus flanked by two 'urinating' boys. Inside the church is a magnificent spiral staircase leading to the 16th-century organ case.

A short distance northeast from the church off rue Martainville is the Aître St-Maclou, a group of 16th-century timber-framed buildings around a courtyard. This was originally the parish charnel-house and now forms part of the Fine Arts School. The galleries are decorated with macabre carvings of skeletons, skulls and other *memento mori*. Immediately right of the entrance, behind a glass panel, is the skeletal mummy of a cat.

TOUR JEANNE D'ARC ✪

Only a massive round donjon, with 4m-thick walls and a witch's-hat roof, survives of the 13th-century fortress built by King Philippe Auguste. The name is slightly misleading: Jeanne d'Arc (Joan of Arc) was imprisoned in another tower and was only brought here to be shown the torture chamber as part of the attempt to break her spirit. The tower now houses documents about Joan's trial along with displays tracing the history of the region.

✚ 34B3
✉ rue du Donjon
☎ 02 35 98 16 21
🕐 Mon–Sat 10–12:30, 2–6 (5 Oct–Mar); Sun 2–6:30 (5:30 Oct–Mar)
🚇 Beaux-Arts
🚌 1, 2, 3, 4, 11, 13, 20, 22
💷 Cheap

A Walk Around Old Rouen

Distance
About 2.5km

Time
1 hour, excluding visits

Start point
Cathédrale Notre-Dame
🚹 34B2
🚌 3, 13

End point
Place du Vieux-Marché
🚹 34B2
🚌 2, 12, 28

Lunch
La Taverne Walsheim (££)
✉ rue Martainville
☎ 02 35 98 27 50

This walk, starting at the cathedral, leads past some of the best architecture of the old town.

Turn right up rue St-Romain.

Medieval buildings are crammed along one side of the street; note Roussel's wrought-iron shopfront. At the archbishop's palace, opposite, Joan of Arc was condemned in 1431 and posthumously declared innocent 25 years later.

At place Barthélemy visit Église St-Maclou (➤ 34); then take rue Martainville and turn left at 186 for Aitre St-Maclou (➤ 35). Return to place Barthélemy and turn right up rue Damiette. Continue to place du Lt–Aubert and detour left up rue d'Amiens.

Spectacular Rubenesque figures and other statues adorn the walls of the Medical Laboratory and the building opposite.

Return to the square and continue along rue des Boucheries–St–Ouen, then turn right up rue Eau–de–Robec, where footbridges cross a narrow stream.

On the right, housed in a splendid medieval building, the Musée de l'Éducation illustrates the upbringing and education of children.

Cross place St–Vivien and continue along rue Eau–de–Robec to rue Édouard–Adam. Turn left and head for place de la Croix de Pierre; then turn left up rue St–Vivien.

Beyond place St-Vivien, the street leads past Église St-Ouen on the right and a huddle of narrow timber-framed houses on the left.

Timbered jetties above rue Martainville, near Église St-Maclou

Continue into rue de l'Hôpital and turn left on to rue des Carmes. Follow this to rue du Gros-Horloge. Turn right and continue under the Gros-Horloge (➤ 26) to place du Vieux-Marché.

What to See in the Northeast

LES ANDELYS AND CHÂTEAU GAILLARD (▶ 17, TOP TEN)

ANET, CHÂTEAU D' ✪✪
In 1531 the future King Henri II, then just 12 years old, fell under the spell of Diane de Poitiers, the beautiful 32-year-old widow of Louis de Brézé, the former Lord of Anet. She became his mistress, and when Henri died in 1559 Diane retired to her château – a glorious showplace. Celebrated craftsmen worked here, including Benvenuto Cellini; Philibert Delorme designed the gateway and its extraordinary clock, with hounds that once barked the hour and a stag that stamped its hoof. Tours include the state rooms and chapel, adorned with golden globes.

ARQUES-LA-BATAILLE ✪
The donjon and walls of an 11th-century fortress dominate this riverside town. The battle referred to in the place name was in 1589, when Protestant Henri IV saw off the superior forces of the Catholic League. Despite the siege and stone robbing the ruins are still impressive; the gatehouse shows a carved relief of the battle. The town's 16th-century Église Notre-Dame de l'Assomption has a bust of Henri IV.

CAUDEBEC-EN-CAUX ✪
Extending along a wide stretch of the Seine, Caudebec has the air of a minor seaside resort, with shops and restaurants lining the waterfront. The Flamboyant Église Notre-Dame stands in the market place amid modern apartment blocks and shops. The **Maison des Templiers**, a 13th-century stone building, houses a local history display, and the Musée de la Marine de Seine looks at river navigation through the ages. Just outside the town the nose and wing of a stone biplane protrude from a rock, a memorial to five aviators who disappeared in the 1920s en route to the Arctic to rescue Italian balloonists who had crashed near Spitzbergen.

Château d'Anet, with the clock gateway on the left

✚ 41B1
☎ 02 37 41 90 07
🕓 Apr–Oct, Mon–Sat 2:30–6:30, Sun and public hols 10–11:30, 2:30–6; Nov–Mar, Sat 2–5, Sun and public hols 10–11:30, 2:30–6:30
🍴 Restaurants in Anet (£–££)
🚌 3 from Dreux
💷 Expensive

✚ 39C2
🍴 Choice in Dieppe (£–£££), or Manoir d'Archelles, south on D1 near Martigny (£–££)
🚌 L5/63 from Dieppe, 15B from Rouen
🚢 Dieppe (▶ 21)

✚ 38B1
🍴 Restaurants (££–£££)
🚌 30 from Rouen, 20 from Le Havre

Maison des Templiers
✉ rue Thomas Basin
☎ 02 39 96 95 91
🕓 Jul–Sep, Wed–Mon 2–6; Apr–Jun, weekend and public hols 2–6
💷 Cheap

37

CLÈRES ✪

A large covered market hall forms the centre of this quiet village, but the main attraction lies to the west where the 19th-century neo-Gothic Château de Clères stands on the site of an 11th-century stronghold. Since 1920 its grounds have been given over to the **Parc Zoologique** whose inhabitants include flamingos, emus, peacocks, kangaroos and antelopes. The Musée de l'Automobile has a collection of vintage cars ranging from the late 19th to the early 20th centuries, as well as cycles and military vehicles from World War II.

DIEPPE (➤ 21, TOP TEN)

ÉCOUIS ✪✪

Planted incongruously in the middle of this unremarkable village is the twin-towered collegiate church of Notre-Dame, visible from afar across the flat countryside. Built in the early 14th century by King Philip IV's finance minister, Enguerrand de Marigny, it has a wonderfully spacious interior lit by two large stained-glass transept windows. Look out for the brick vault and intricately carved bosses in the side chapel, carved doors and wooden ceiling in the enclosed chapel near the entrance, and timber spiral stairs leading to the organ loft.

Exotic cranes wander freely on the lawns around the Château de Clères

NORTHEAST NORMANDY

ÉTRETAT ✪✪✪

Étretat is the most attractive Norman resort north of Honfleur and is always busy in summer. Out of season it carries on a quiet but cheerful life of its own.

The shingle beach stretches between two glaring chalk headlands, both sculpted by the elements. The Falaise d'Aval (western cliff) ends in a wide and fragile-looking arch, a flying buttress against the main body of rock. The eastern cliff, the Falaise d'Amont, is less dramatic. Perched on top of it is the seamen's chapel of Notre-Dame-de-la-Garde, and a monument commemorating Charles Nungesser and François Coli, French aviators who set out from Paris in 1927 to try and cross the Atlantic to New York in their 'Oiseau Blanc'; they were last seen over this part of the coast. There is also a museum with mementoes of the pilots.

The centre of the town is full of character. In place du Maréchal Foch 16th-century town houses are grouped around the wooden *halles* (covered market), where in summer souvenir shops open under the first-floor galleries; over the entrance to the *halles* is an unusual carving of a bat with a man's head. A plaque beneath the clock tower in the *place* commemorates Étretat's World War I field hospital, and the arrival of Scottish troops in World War II.

➕ 38A2
🍴 Choice of restaurants (£–£££)
↔ Fécamp (► 40)

The natural chalk arch of the Falaise d'Aval
Insert: *aviators Nungesser and Coli*

39D3
Hôtel de la Gare, 20
avenue de la Gare (£–££)
15B from Rouen/Dieppe
Le Tréport (▶ 45)

Musée Louis-Philippe
02 35 86 44 00
Mid-Mar to 5 Nov,
Wed–Mon 10–12, 2–6
Good
Moderate

38A2
Choice of restaurants on
quays (£–££)
60/61 from Dieppe, 26B
from Rouen
7 a day from Rouen
Étretat (▶ 39)

Palais Bénédictine
110 rue Alexandre-le-
Grand
02 35 10 26 10
Guided tours: Mar–May,
10–12, 2–5:30; Jun–early
Sep, 9:30–6; early Sep to
mid-Nov, mid-Nov to Feb,
10:30 and
3:30
Few
Moderate

EU ✪

Set on the Bresle river, with the Forêt d'Eu spreading towards the southeast, this once powerful *ville royale* has two buildings out of proportion to the small centre. The grandiose red-brick and stone Château d'Eu, on the site of an older fortress where William the Conqueror was married, was the favoured home of King Louis-Philippe and houses the **Musée Louis-Philippe**. Facing it is the medieval Église Notre-Dame et St-Laurent that houses the remains of Saint Laurence O'Toole, a 12th-century archbishop of Dublin.

FÉCAMP ✪✪

This workaday harbour town is the home of Bénédictine liqueur, made from a secret recipe discovered by Alexandre le Grand in a 16th-century monastic manuscript. Le Grand promoted the product with gusto, commissioning posters by celebrated artists and building the neo-Gothic **Palais Bénédictine**. This now contains an art gallery and museum, as well as the copper Bénédictine stills; tours and tastings are provided.

For centuries Fécamp was a major centre of pilgrimage and people flocked to the monastery to see the relic of the Precious Blood of Christ; it was supposedly washed ashore in a hollow fig tree and is now housed in the beautiful 12th- to 13th-century Église de La Trinité.

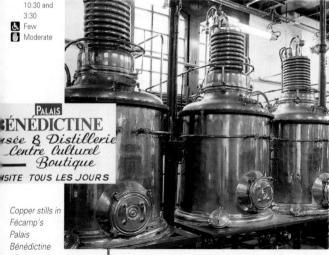

Copper stills in Fécamp's Palais Bénédictine

Did you know ?

*Eu was an important administrative town
until the 15th century, when Louis XI took
drastic action to prevent its fall into English
hands. He had everything bar the churches
burned to the ground, and the town
never recovered its former glory.*

GISORS ✪

The capital of the Normandie-Vexin stands on rising ground
beside the region's eastern border, amid seemingly
endless flatlands. Behind the main street are the ruins of a
12th-century fortress, whose slender donjon was built by
King Henry II of England; it is surrounded by moss-covered
walls and a filled-in ditch where locals now play *boules*.
King Philippe Auguste added the Tour du Prisonnier, which
became a prison in the 16th century – drawings and
inscriptions by the inmates can still be seen. Across town
the church of St-Gervais and St-Protais contains an
impressive Tree of Jesse.

✚ 41C3
🍴 Choice of restaurants
(££–£££)
🚌 2 a day from Évreux

SEINE VALLEY

Reflections on the water-lily pond at Giverny

GIVERNY ✪✪

Visitors come to this riverside hamlet to see Claude Monet's house and the gardens that he created and later painted (▶ 14). Footpaths lead round the gardens, which are very beautiful but inevitably obscured by the crowds. The most popular photo opportunity is the water-lily pond and its bridge, familiar from Monet's famous series of paintings. A road through the **Jardins Monet** divides the Clos Normand (enclosed garden) from the Water Garden. The artist's 'pink house' has reproductions of his works, Japanese engravings, and rooms decorated in different colours. The Musée d'Art Américain, near by, celebrates the works of American artists past and present.

LE HAVRE ✪

From the Pont de Normandie and the east traffic enters Le Havre past petrochemical factories into a maze of low apartment blocks and shops. This is the modern centre designed by Auguste Perret after the old town was levelled in World War II. One of the few pre-war survivors is the 17th-century building housing the **Musée de l'Ancien Havre**, a token of the town's former character.

Le Havre has a long seafaring pedigree, but rather than try to recapture the past Perret went for unapologetic modernism. Beyond the *bassin du commerce* (commercial dock), crossed by an elegant white bridge, a ship's funnel rises from the underground bowl of Espace Oscar Niemeyer, home of Le Volcan arts centre. Inside Perret's monumental Église St-Joseph to the west, light sparkles through the stained glass of the 109m octagonal lantern tower to the semi-darkness within. To the south, the 16th-century Cathédrale Notre-Dame is an eccentric mix of architectural styles.

HONFLEUR (► 23, TOP TEN)

JUMIÈGES, ABBAYE DE (► 16, TOP TEN)

LYONS-LA-FORÊT

Huddled in a dip of the Lieure Valley, Lyons-la-Forêt is a classic Norman timber-framed village, where narrow 17th-century buildings crowd round the old *halles*. A wonderful old house downhill from the market square, topped with decorative ceramic chimney pots, has a plaque stating that Maurice Ravel composed *Le Tombeau de Couperin* there in 1917. These houses and the 12th-century Église St-Denis are the only sights as such, but the prettiness of this picture-postcard village makes it a popular base for exploring the surrounding Forêt de Lyons.

Among the slender beeches – which filter an ethereal light even into the heart of the forest – is the Abbaye de Mortemer, ruins of a medieval Cistercian abbey with a museum of monastic life. Here also are the **Château de Fleury-la-Forêt** with its collection of toys and dolls, and the Château de Vascœuil on the forest's edge, with reconstructions of traditional cottages in its grounds.

- 39D1
- La Licorne (££–£££)
- 28 from Rouen
- Écouis (► 38)

Château de Fleury-la-Forêt
- D13, 6km northeast of Lyons-la-Forêt
- 02 32 49 54 36
- Jul–Aug, guided tours daily 2–6; Sep–Jun, weekend and public hols 2–6
- Expensive; moderate for grounds only

The timber halles *at Lyons-la-Forêt*

MARTAINVILLE, CHÂTEAU DE

Privateer Jacques le Pelletier built this château in the late 15th century, and his nephew later transformed it from a fortified house into a stately home. Its round, red-brick towers are topped with conical roofs and there is a large 16th-century dovecote in the grounds. Inside is the Musée Départemental des Traditions et Arts Normands, with a collection of furniture, ceramics, glass and costumes.

- 41A3
- 16km east of Rouen
- 02 35 23 44 70
- Wed–Mon 10–12:30, 2–6 (till 5 in winter)
- Restaurants in village (££)
- 28A from Rouen
- Moderate

MIROMESNIL, CHÂTEAU DE

Guy de Maupassant (1850–93) was born in this 16th-century red-brick and stone château. Memorabilia associated with the writer are displayed inside, as well as books collected by the Marquis de Miromesnil, Louis XVI's chancellor, who died here in 1796. A 16th-century chapel with an ornate interior stands in the grounds.

- 39C2
- Tourville-sur-Arques
- 02 35 80 02 80
- May to mid-Oct, guided tours Wed–Mon 2–6
- From Dieppe (summer)
- Expensive

38B1

Choice of cafés and restaurants (£–££)

31 from Lisieux or Rouen

Goods change hands at Pont-Audemer's busy market

PONT-AUDEMER ✪✪

Pont-Audemer's prosperity was built on its tanneries, and it retains the air of a working town. Situated between two branches of the Risle river, the modern shops and houses blend with narrow alleyways and court-yards lined with historic buildings. Canals cut through town, crossed by wooden footbridges, and there are good examples of 17th-century housing along rue de la République, Cour Canel and near the 11th-century Église St-Ouen.

39C1

10km northwest of Rouen off D982

02 35 32 10 82

Bars near the church (£)

30 from Rouen

Few; difficult access to church

Moderate

ST-MARTIN-DE-BOSCHERVILLE ✪✪

This tiny village is dominated by the former abbey church, now the parish church of St-Georges-de-Boscherville. Refounded as a Benedictine monastery in 1144, it housed a small community of monks until they fled during the Revolution. Wide steps ascend to the church's simple Romanesque façade, built of gleaming limestone with a fine doorway. Inside, the space and light created by its austere design is breathtaking; look for the puppet-like carvings on the transept columns.

38B1

30km west of Rouen, off D982

02 35 96 23 11

Guided tours of cloisters daily 3 and 4; also 11:30 Sun and public hols

Auberge Deux Couronnes (££); tearooms in village (££)

30 from Rouen

None

Moderate (for tour)

Caudebec-en-Caux (➤ 37)

Visitors are asked not to talk loudly

Benedictine monks enter the precinct of St-Wandrille

ST-WANDRILLE, ABBAYE DE ✪

In 628 Count Wandrille renounced the secular world and after stops at various monasteries founded his own in the Seine Valley. It soon gained a reputation for scholarship but had to be rebuilt after Viking raids. The abbey passed into private hands after the French Revolution until 1931 when the Benedictine community was re-established. Remains of the 14th-century abbey church and cloister can be seen in the grounds, as well as a 13th-century tithe barn rebuilt by the monks in 1967.

The impressive columns of the Abbaye de St-Wandrille tower above visitors

LE TRÉPORT ✪

The bracing seaside resort of le Tréport lies on the region's windswept northeastern corner. High chalk cliffs shelter a shingle beach and provide views from the Calvaire des Terrasses. The restored 16th-century Église St-Jacques at the end of quai François 1er overlooks the harbour and fishing boats; its 11th-century predecessor disappeared with former cliffs into the sea.

✚ 39D3
🍴 Choice of cafés and seafood restaurants along quai François 1er (££)
🚌 15B from Rouen and Dieppe
🚆 Eu (▶ 40)

VALMONT ✪

From the flint and brick church at the centre of this small country town you can look up at the high, buttressed walls and slate roofs of the château established by the powerful Estouteville family. In 1169 Nicolas d'Estouteville founded the Benedictine **abbey** whose ruins stand at the foot of a wooded slope. They include the 16th-century choir, and the graceful Chapelle de la Vierge, or Six Heures (the time of the daily mass), that houses the tombs of Jacques d'Estouteville and the abbey's founder; five 15th-century windows depict the life of the Virgin.

✚ 38B2
🍴 Auberge du Bec au Cauchois, 1.5km west (£–££)
🚌 26B from Rouen

Abbaye
☎ 02 35 27 34 92
🕐 Guided tours: Apr–Sep, Wed–Mon
🎫 Cheap

A Drive Along the Côte d'Albâtre

Distance
80km

Time
2½ hours excluding visits

Start point
Dieppe
 39C2

End point
Étretat
38A2

Lunch
Hôtel des Bains
brasserie/restaurant (£–££)
✉ 15 place du Marché, St-
Valéry-en-Caux
☎ 02 35 97 04 32

This coastal drive detours inland to explore the Pays de Caux.

From Dieppe take the D75 signed St-Valéry-en-Caux.

The road twists down into the breezy resort of Pourville-sur-Mer, with panoramic sea views.

Continue along the D75 through Varengeville-sur-Mer (➤ 47) to Ste-Marguerite-sur-Mer.

Stop here to look at the 12th- to 16th-century church. To the right of the entrance is a carving of an owl holding a snake in its beak; owl motifs are repeated on columns in the dark interior.

At St-Aubin-sur-Mer follow the coast to Veules-les-Roses; turn right on to the D925 (St-Valéry-en-Caux). Take the D925 towards Fécamp and turn on to the D68 (signed St-Sylvain). The road passes through a broad, flat landscape with an aerodrome in the distance, before descending through beech woods into Paluel. Continue to St-Martin-aux-Buneaux and take the D68 to Sassetot-le-Mauconduit.

High and dry on the beach near Yport

At Malleville-les-Grès, beyond Paluel, the D68 passes a handsome manor house and a 1650 stone cross. Next, a turreted wall surrounds the lordly 15th-century château at Auberville-la-Manuel. Facing the road at Sassetot is a pink and white château, now a hotel.

Follow signs to Valmont (➤ 45). Take the D150 to Fécamp (➤ 40), then the D940 and D104 to Yport. From Yport, with its impressive red-brick and limestone church, the D211 winds through woodland, overlooking the sea, to Vattetot-sur-Mer. At Vattetot turn right on to the D11 and descend into a green valley on the approach to Étretat.

VARENGEVILLE-SUR-MER ✪

The wooded coast road runs southwest of Dieppe through a series of townships that make up Varengeville. Just inland the privateer-politician Jean Ango built his summer palace, the **Manoir d'Ango**, in 1530, decorating it with busts of the great and good, including François I and himself.

Closer to the coast, the gardens of the **Parc Floral du Bois des Moutiers** include rhododendrons and magnolias among the shrubs offering spring colour. Formal flower beds are arranged around a house built in 1898 from the designs of the English architect Edwin Lutyens. In the town's clifftop church is a stunning stained-glass Tree of Jesse by Georges Braque; the cubist painter came to live here in 1930.

🚩	39C2
🍴	Hôtel de la Terrasse (£–££)
🚌	60/61 from Dieppe
🚆	Dieppe (➤ 21)

Manoir d'Ango
✉	7km west of Dieppe
☎	02 35 85 14 80
🕐	Mar–Nov, weekend and public hols 10–12:30, 2:30–6:30
💰	Moderate

Parc Floral du Bois des Moutiers
✉	78km west of Dieppe
☎	02 35 85 10 02
🕐	Mid-Mar to mid-Nov, daily 10–12, 2–6
💰	Expensive for tours of gardens plus house

Braque's vivid Tree of Jesse window in the church at Varengeville

VERNON ✪

Vernon is a bustling market town on the Seine. Many of its medieval buildings survive, one of the best, with faded 15th-century carvings, housing the tourist office on rue Carnot; the nearby Gothic church has striking abstract stained-glass windows. The massive circular donjon visible from the rue du Vieux Château was once part of the castle built by King Philippe Auguste. Across the river, near the miniature Château des Tourelles, a timber-framed house perches on a stump of the former medieval bridge.

Just outside Vernon the 18th-century **Château de Bizy**, set in terraced gardens, has a fine collection of tapestries.

🚩	41B2
🍴	Restaurants (£–£££)
🚌	From Évreux

Château de Bizy
✉	2km south of Vernon
☎	02 32 51 00 82
🕐	Apr–Oct, Tue–Sun 10–12, 2–6; Nov, Feb–Mar, weekend 2–5. Closed Dec–Jan
💰	Expensive

Caen & Central Normandy

Central Normandy is composed of a variety of landscapes, from the D-Day beaches and seaside resorts of the Côte Fleurie and the Côte de Nacre, to the quiet towns of the rural south.

Between the coast and the distant Loire region are the lush fields, dairy farms and orchards of the Pays d'Auge around Lisieux, the gentle Pays d'Ouche south of Bernay, and the rich meadows of the Perche region, famous for its horses. To the the west, the rocky gorges and wooded hills of the Suisse Normande are perfect for hiking, walking and canoeing.

As well as the traditional timber-framed buildings, there are churches and houses of mellow, creamy limestone; this same material was once shipped from the busy port of Caen to build new cathedrals in the Norman-ruled kingdom of England.

> *' … the most prepossessing*
> *… and most happily*
> *situated of towns … and*
> *from this town have come*
> *the brightest wits and*
> *intelligences of their*
> *country. '*

MADAME DE SÉVIGNÉ,
of Caen in 1689

———————•———————

Opposite: *Abbaye aux Hommes, Caen*

CENTRAL NORMANDY

Baie de la Seine

Côte de Nacre

Côte

Grandcamp-Maisy
Pointe du Hoc
Vierville-sur-Mer
Omaha Beach
Port-en-Bessin
Gold Beach
Courseulles-sur-Mer
St-Aubin-sur-Mer
Luc-sur-Mer
Dives-sur-Mer
Isigny-sur-Mer
St-Laurent-sur-Mer
la Cambe
Aure
Arromanches-les-Bains
St-Gabriel-Brécy
Riva-Bella
Sword Beach
Cabourg
Carentan
Bayeux
Brécy
Château de Fontaine Henry
Ouistreham
Pégasus Bridge
Bénouville
Abbaye Cérisy-la-Forêt
Abbaye d'Ardenne
le Mémorial
Balleroy
Tilly-sur-Seulles
CAEN
Troarn
Vire
St-Lô
Caumont-l'Éventé
Orne
Château du Canon
Roches de Ham
Torigni-sur-Vire
Villers-Bocage
Vendeuvre
Tessy-sur-Vire
Aunay-sur-Odon
Thury-Harcourt
Suisse
Dives
Percy
Pont-Farcy
le Bény-Bocage
Normande
Villedieu-les-Poêles
Château de Pontécoulant
Clécy
Aubigny
Falaise
St-Sever-Calvados
Vire
Vassy
Condé-sur-Noireau
Roche d'Oëtre
Forêt de
Brécey
Sée
Tinchebray
Flers
Orne
Argentan
Juvigny-le-Tertre
Sourdeval
Fromentel
l'Abbaye Blanche
Mortain
Briouze
St-Hilaire-du-Harcouët
Barenton
Domfront
Rânes
Château de Sassy
Sélune
le Teilleul
la Ferté-Macé
Landivy
Bagnoles-de-l'Orne
Carrouges
Couterne
Lassay-les-Châteaux
Couptrain
Gorron
Pré-en-Pail
417m Mt des Avaloirs
Fougères
Ambrières-les-Vallées
Javron-les-Chapelles
Alpes
Mancelles
Ernée
Villaines-la-Juhel
Sarthe
Mayenne
St-Léonard-des-Bois
Mayenne
Bais
Juvigné
Ernée

Cap de la Hève
Harfleur
Caudebec-en-Caux
St-Wandrille
Barentin
Château d'Orcher
LE HAVRE
Lillebonne
Tancarville
Château d'Etelan
Honfleur
Pont de Tancarville
Pont de Normandie
Seine
Jumièges
ROUEN
Bourneville
Fleurie
Villerville
Trouville-sur-Mer
St-Maclou
Deauville
Canapville
Beuzeville
Villers-sur-Mer
Bourg-Achard
Touques
Bourgtheroulde-Infreville
Château de Robert-le-Diable
Houlgate
Pont-l'Évêque
Pont-Audemer
Cormeilles
Elbeuf
Dozulé
Lieurey
le Bec-Hellouin
Heuvron-en-Auge
Risle
Cambremer
Brionne
Louviers
Crèvecoeur-en-Auge
Lisieux
Harcourt
Château du Champ-de-Bataille
St-Germain-de-Livet
Bernay
Serquigny
le Neubourg
Auge
Vie
Beaumont-le-Roger
St-Pierre-sur-Dives
Livarot
Orbec
Broglie
Charentonne
Beaumesnil
Evreux
Vimoutiers
Courteilles
Risle
Conches-en-Ouche
Camembert
la Neuve-Lyre
Iton
Trun
Pays   d'Ouche
Damville
Chambois
Rugles
Breteuil
le Bourg-St-Léonard
Abbaye St-Evroult-Notre-Dame-du-Bois
Gouffern
Gacé
l'Aigle
St-Lubin-des-Joncherets
le Pin-au-Haras
Aube
Verneuil-sur-Avre
Nonant-le-Pin
Ste-Gauburge-Ste-Colombe
Médavy
Avre
Brézolles
Château d'O
Moulins-la-Marche
Randonnai
Mortrée
Courtomer
Abbaye de la Trappe
la Ferté-Vidame
Sées
Forêt d'Ecouves
Bazoches-sur-Hoëne
Senonches
Rocher du Vignage
Mortagne-au-Perche
Longny-au-Perche
Forêt de Réno Valdieu
Eure
la Loupe
Alençon
Manoir de la Vove
Rémalard
Forêt de Perseigne
Forêt de Bellême
Huisne
Bellême
la Hutte
Mamers
Nogent-le-Rotrou
Fresnay-sur-Sarthe
Beaumont-sur-Sarthe
Luigny

0   10   20   30 km

D   E   F

Some of the older houses that survived the battle for Caen during June and July 1944

Caen

Traffic roars around Caen's floodlit medieval château, which, along with the Église St-Pierre opposite its town gate, provides the main focus of this busy river port. Three-quarters of the city were destroyed during World War II, but the modern, businesslike centre still retains a few old buildings in golden Caen limestone. On the outskirts, the cost and legacy of war are considered in the remarkable Mémorial (▶ 19).

What to See in Caen

 50C4

 place de la Reine Mathilde
☎ 02 31 06 98 98
🕐 Guided tours: daily 2:30, 4. Closed 1 Jan, 1 May, 25 Dec
♿ Good
🎟 Free

ABBAYE AUX DAMES   ✪

Duke William, later Conqueror, defied a papal ruling to marry his distant cousin, Matilda of Flanders, and both were excommunicated in 1051. Eight years later, Abbot Lanfranc of Bec persuaded the Pope to lift the exclusion in return for the founding of two abbeys: the Abbaye aux Dames, northeast of the centre, where Matilda would be interred, and the Abbaye aux Hommes, William's mausoleum. Matilda's simple black-marble tomb lies in the chancel of the abbey church, La Trinité.

 esplanade Jean-Marie Louvel
☎ 02 31 30 42 81
🕐 Guided tours: daily 9:30, 11, 2:30, 4. Closed 1 Jan, 1 May, 25 Dec
♿ None
🎟 Cheap

ABBAYE AUX HOMMES   ✪✪

Viewed from the east across a geometric formal garden, the abbey buildings and Église St-Étienne present a striking mixture of styles. To the left are the classical 18th-century monastic buildings, now housing the town hall; to the right the chancel of the abbey church, busy with early Gothic spires, turrets and buttresses. The original west façade is simpler, its elegant 11th-century towers crowned in the 13th century with octagonal spires. The Conqueror's fragmentary remains – one thigh bone – lie under an inscribed stone by the altar; the rest were stolen when Huguenots raided the church in the 16th century.

CHÂTEAU ✪✪

Another of Duke William's foundations, the château was strengthened and embellished over several centuries. Its massive donjon was only destroyed during the Revolution, and more followed during World War II, but the restored walls are still impressive, situated on a rocky eminence surrounded by a grassed-over moat. Within the walls are the **Musée des Beaux-Arts** with its fine collection of 16th- to 17th-century Flemish, French and Italian paintings, and the **Musée de Normandie** (in the former governor's residence) that traces the region's history.

🖂 rue Montoir-Poissonnerie, entry through Porte sur la Ville
🏛 Free

Musée des Beaux-Arts
🖂 Château precinct
☎ 02 31 30 47 70
🕐 Wed–Mon 10–6. Closed 1 Jan, Easter, 1 May, Ascension, 11 Nov, 25 Dec
♿ Good, some sections inaccessible
🎫 Moderate; free Wed

Musée de Normandie
🖂 Château precinct
☎ 02 31 30 47 50
🕐 Apr–Sep, Wed–Fri 10–12:30, 1.30–6, Sat–Mon 9:30–12:30, 2–6; Oct–Mar, Wed–Mon 9:30–12:30, 2–6
♿ None
🎫 Cheap; free Wed

The restored 12th-century walls of Caen's mighty château

ST-PIERRE, ÉGLISE ✪✪

St-Pierre's 72m spire provides a useful landmark within the town's confusing road system. There has been a church on the site since the 7th century, but the present building is mainly 13th- to 16th-century. There are some fine carvings inside, particularly on the columns on the northern side of the nave; medieval scenes here include a phoenix rising from the ashes, a unicorn comforted by a young woman, and the trials of the Knights of the Round Table.

🖂 rue Montoir-Poissonnerie
🍴 Choice of restaurants, cafés and bars (£–£££)

53

A Walk Around Caen's Monuments

Distance
About 5km

Time
1½ hours without visits

Start point
Abbaye aux Dames

End point
Abbaye aux Hommes

Lunch
L'Amandier (£–££)
✉ rue Froide
☎ 02 31 85 33 39

Fourteenth-century vaulting in the Église St-Pierre, rebuilt after the devastation of 1944

This walk takes you from Mathilde's resting-place, Abbaye aux Dames, to that of William the Conqueror, visiting the main monuments and streets between the mausoleum churches.

Leaving the abbey church of La Trinité (place de la Reine Mathilde, ► 52), turn left and go down rue Manissier. At the end turn right on to rue Basse and continue to the pedestrian crossing; then turn left (rue Samuel Bochard) to reach place Courtonne.

Hotels and restaurants line this large open square that takes in the yachting marina and port at one end, and the lone Tour Guillaume-le-Roy at the other.

Turn right along rue des Prairies St-Gilles to rejoin rue Basse, then right up rue Buquet. Cross into rue du Vaugueux.

Some of Caen's most atmospheric restaurants can be found in this secluded cobbled area, one of the few surviving old streets.

At the end of the street cross the road to the castle: enter the grounds over the long drawbridge. Exit from the Musée des Beaux-Arts to Église St-Pierre (► 53), and cross into rue St-Pierre.

The Musée de la Poste, on this bustling shopping street, occupies the best example of timber-framed architecture in the city centre .

Just beyond the Église St-Sauveur (also known as Notre-Dame de Froide-rue), turn right into rue Froide. Continue to rue St-Sauveur and (left) place St-Sauveur.

Elegant town houses lead from Vieux St-Sauveur, a medieval church gradually being restored after extensive wartime damage, to the Palais de Justice whose classical columns dominate place Fontette.

Cross the square to the formal gardens for a magnificent view of Duke William's Abbaye aux Hommes (► 52).

What to See in Central Normandy

ALENÇON ✪

Alençon is a pleasant, unspoiled town of narrow streets and squares, whose centre is dominated by the neo-classical Palais de Justice and the grim château gatehouse. The nearby market hall is a striking circular, glass-domed building. The town made a name for itself when Louis XIV's minister Colbert established a lace industry here. Samples of Alençon lace are shown in the Musée des Beaux-Arts et de la Dentelle, a former Jesuit college.

➕ 51D1
🍴 Choice of restaurants (££)
🚌 2 from Argentan
🚂 4 a day from Rouen, Cherbourg
↔ Carrouges (► 61), Mortagne-au-Perche (► 67), Sées (► 74)

ARGENTAN ✪

Argentan provides a good touring centre for excursions into the wooded Suisse Normande. The town itself, which once rivalled Alençon's lace industry, has an impressive Flamboyant church – St-Germain – that stands opposite the turreted 14th-century château (now housing law courts); standing apart from the château is its former chapel, now the tourist information centre. The town was the scene of historic talks in the late 12th century, with papal legates trying to reconcile King Henry II of England and Thomas à Becket; when they failed, Henry's knights set off from Argentan to rid him of his 'turbulent priest'.

➕ 50C3
🍴 Restaurants in town (£–££)
🚌 2 from Alençon
🚂 4 a day from Rouen, 4 a day from Granville (Paris Montparnasse–Granville line)
↔ Château d'O (► 20), Château de Sassy (► 73)

ARROMANCHES-LES-BAINS ✪✪

Fragments of the artificial harbour 'Mulberry B' form a vast semicircle in the sea beyond this quiet seaside resort, a reminder of the D-Day landings of June 1944. It was one of two concrete breakwaters towed to France to allow the landing of troops and 500,000 tons of equipment. Chunks of the harbour also lie on the sandy beach, giving an idea of the sheer size and scale of the operation, an account of which is given in the Musée du Débarquement.

➕ 50B5
🍴 Choice of cafés and brasseries (£–££)
🚌 74 from Bayeux
↔ Bayeux (► 18, 57)

Above: *remains of the Mulberry harbour lie offshore at Arromanches*

A Drive Through Southern Forests

Distance
About 205km

Time
3½–4 hours without stops

Start/end point
Alençon
🚩 51D1

Lunch
Hostellerie Genty-Home
(£–££)
✉ 4 rue Notre-Dame,
Mortagne-au-Perche
☎ 02 33 25 11 53

This long circular drive passes through the Parc Naturel Régional Normandie-Maine and southern Normandy's ancient forests.

From Alençon, take the D311 east through the Forêt de Perseigne. At the roundabout before Mamers follow signs for Bellême (D311/D955).

Beyond the woods the road leads through gentle countryside into the Perche, with its extensive fields and pasture.

At the roundabout before Bellême turn left on to the D938 through the Forêt de Bellême, heading north to Mortagne–au–Perche. Beyond Mortagne's market hall turn right (D8).

The route passes through hamlets, pastureland and the Forêt de Réno-Valdieu to Longny-au-Perche. Here, a long flight of steps leads to the 16th-century Chapelle de Notre-Dame de Pitié, and the 16th-century tower of Église St-Martin overlooks the central square.

In the centre turn left (D918) to pass through the Forêt du Perche to Randonnai. Turn left at the traffic lights (D603).

The road leads between the Forêts du Perche and de la Trappe; a series of lakes can be glimpsed through the trees. A crucifix stands above the road as it reaches a fork. Take the right fork (Rond de Trappe), but be careful: deer are still hunted here.

Emerging on to the D930, turn right, then first left to the Abbaye de la Trappe.

Founded in 1140, the abbey has an audio-visual display describing the life of Trappist monks.

One of the peaceful roads that weave through the forests of Normandy

Turn left on a minor road to Prépotin; then left to a T-junction and right (D930). Turn right on to the N12. At the roundabout join the D8 to Sées (▶ 74). Take the D908 to a crossroads and turn left (D26) through the Forêt d'Écouves and back to Alençon.

BALLEROY, CHÂTEAU DE ✪

A long tree-lined road leads through Balleroy to this early 17th-century mansion overlooking the Drôme Valley. The symmetrical pink and grey château, built by François Mansart for Jean de Choisy, was bought in 1970 by the American publishing magnate Malcolm Forbes. His passion for ballooning inspired the Musée des Ballons that traces the sport's history from the first passenger flight in 1783 to barrage balloons of World War II.

✚ 50B4
✉ 15km southwest of Bayeux, off D572
☎ 02 31 21 60 61
🕐 Mid-Mar to mid-Oct, Wed–Mon 9–12, 2–6; Jul–Aug daily 10–6
🚌 71/73 from Bayeux
💰 Expensive

BAYEUX ✪✪✪

Bayeux's chief attraction is its tapestry (➤ 18), yet the town itself has great charm. An air of quiet prosperity hangs over its old stone and timber-framed buildings; the Aure river flows past watermills, and the cathedral forms a graceful focus. Built by Odo – sponsor of the tapestry – the cathedral still has its original towers and crypt. The nave's 12th-century arcades are decorated with Romanesque and oriental designs, and interesting frescos include a portrayal of Thomas à Becket's murder, while angels play musical instruments in the crypt. Beside the cathedral, the Musée Baron Gérard includes porcelain, furniture and paintings. The **Musée Mémorial de la Bataille de Normandie 1944** presents a vivid picture of the Battle of Normandy.

✚ 50B5
🍴 Choice of restaurants on rue St-Jean (£–£££)
🚌 30 from Caen
🚆 6 a day from Cherbourg, 12 a day from Caen
↔ Caen (➤ 52–54), Arromanches (➤ 55), Cérisy-la-Forêt (➤ 62)

Musée Mémorial de la Bataille de Normandie 1944
✉ boulevard Fabian Ware
☎ 02 31 92 93 41
🕐 May to mid-Sep, 9:30–6:30; mid-Sep to Apr, 10–12:30, 2–6. Closed 25 Dec, 1 Jan, mid-Jan–1 Feb
♿ Very good
💰 Moderate

The cathedral of Bayeux, original showplace of the tapestry

57

✠ 51E4

✉ 13km southeast of
Bernay by D140

☎ 02 32 44 40 09

🕐 Jul–Aug, Wed–Mon
10–12, 2–6; Easter–Jun,
Sep, Fri–Mon 2–6

🍴 L'Etape Louis XIII
(££–£££), in village

👆 Expensive

✠ 51F4

🍴 Restaurants and cafés in
town (£–££)

🚌 37 from Évreux to
Louviers; local buses
from Louviers

🚂 5 a day from Évreux

♿ None

🔄 Château de Beaumesnil
(► above), Bernay (► 59)

---

*Tour St-Nicolas, lone
survivor of the great
medieval abbey of le Bec-
Hellouin*

✠ 51E4

✉ 23km northeast of
Bernay, on D130

☎ 02 32 43 72 60

🕐 Wed–Mon. Guided tours:
Jun–Sep, Mon, Wed–Fri
10, 11, 3, 4, 5; Sat 10, 11,
3, 4; Sun and public hols
12, 3, 4; Oct–May, Mon,
Wed–Fri 11, 3:15, 4:30,
Sun 12, 3, 4

🍴 Restaurants in village
(£–£££)

🚌 24 from Évreux

👆 Moderate

❓ Occasional concerts

58

BEAUMESNIL, CHÂTEAU DE   ✪✪

Behind the hamlet of Beaumesnil this 17th-century red-brick and stone château appears suddenly amid formal gardens, guarded by iron gates and railings. All that remains of the medieval fortress that once stood here is the overgrown base of its donjon. The later building has fashionable Flemish designs, and the grounds were laid out by La Quintinie, a student of André Le Nôtre. The interior contains a fine library, period furniture and a museum of bookbinding.

BEAUMONT-LE-ROGER   ✪

Situated on the edge of the Forêt de Beaumont, the walls of the priory ruins rise like a cliff from the roadside. Roger de Vieilles founded the Prieuré de la Sainte Trinité in 1070 near his castle, but the present remains are 13th-century. A steep path climbs under a series of arches to the hilltop ruins of the nave, with its wide eastern arch and a blind arcade along the length of the north wall. After the priory fell into disuse in the 1780s its relics were taken to the late medieval Église St-Nicolas near by.

BEC-HELLOUIN, ABBAYE DU   ✪✪

This walled Benedictine abbey in the tranquil Risle Valley was once a powerful religious, scholarly and political centre. The first two Norman archbishops of Canterbury, Lanfranc and Anselm, came from Bec; the abbey also produced many other influential churchmen, some of whom are listed on the 15th-century Tour St-Nicolas. In the new abbey church is the tomb of the anchorite Herluin who founded the community in 1034; Lanfranc arrived eight years later having abandoned his teaching at Avranches. The monks fled during the French Revolution, but in 1948 a new community was re-established here – though not before the vast abbey church had been demolished (its foundations can still be seen opposite the tower, the only part to survive).

BERNAY ⭐

Bernay's 11th-century abbey was founded by Judith of Brittany, wife of Duke Richard II, and its church still dominates this substantial country town where tributaries of the Charentonne wind among the streets. The interior of the early Romanesque church has carved capitals in the choir showing animals and foliage in the style of manuscript illuminations. Cars park opposite the apse, which is strikingly decorated with wooden tiles, and the abbey gardens lead to the **Musée Municipal** in the former abbot's lodge, with its collection of art, sculpture and furniture. The town hall occupies the old abbey buildings beside the remains of the 13th-century cloisters. The Église Ste-Croix, on rue Alexandre, houses the tombstones of past abbots and of Guillaume d'Auvillars, a 15th-century abbot of le Bec-Hellouin.

BEUVRON-EN-AUGE ⭐⭐

Set in the heart of the Pays d'Auge, surrounded by orchards, stud farms and grazing cattle, Beuvron-en-Auge must be one of Normandy's prettiest villages. Timber-framed town houses surround the central square, where the steep-roofed *halles* (covered market) contain the Pavé d'Auge restaurant (▶ 97). At the edge of the village the Vieux Manoir, with its cross-braced timbers, is decorated with woodcarvings of faces and figures.

🚩 51E4
🍴 Restaurants, bars in town
🚌 30 from Pont-Audemer
🚃 6 a day from Lisieux, 5 a day from Évreux
↔ Château de Beaumesnil, Beaumont-le-Roger (▶ 58)

Musée Municipal
✉ place Guillaume de Volpiano
☎ 02 32 46 63 23
🕐 Wed–Mon 10–12, 2–5:30 (till 7 from last weekend Jun–first week Sep, and Easter hol); Sun and public hols 3–5:30
💷 Cheap

🚩 50C4
🍴 Auberge de la Boule d'Or (£–££), Pavé d'Auge (££–£££)
↔ Crèvecœur-en-Auge (▶ 63)

The Vieux Manoir, Beuvron-en-Auge

51E4

Restaurants and bars in town (£–££)

24 from Évreux

5 a day from Rouen/Caen

Abbaye du Bec-Hellouin (▶ 59)

BRIONNE ✪

Brionne's importance as a strategic town goes back to the 11th century. Duke William laid siege to it between 1047 and 1050, eventually chasing out the duke of Burgundy. On a hill overlooking the town and the Risle Valley are the massive walls of a ruined 12th-century donjon. The slate-spired Église St-Martin is mainly 15th-century.

About 7km east of Brionne, an agricultural school occupies the moated Château d'Harcourt, set in extensive parkland and originally built for Robert of Harcourt, a companion of King Richard I of England.

51E4

Restaurants and bars in town

Bernay (▶ 59)

BROGLIE ✪✪

Broglie is a small rural town in the wooded Charentonne Valley. The 18th-century château (private) looms above the town on the site of an older fortress, and timber-framed houses crowd around the 12th-century Église St-Martin, built of contrasting conglomerate and limestone with later timber additions. Behind the church is an old house whose timbers are carved with dragons and the weathered face of a green man. Plaques commemorate two of Broglie's distinguished sons: Jean-François Merimée, born here in 1757 and later secretary of the École Nationale des Beaux-Arts; and civil engineer Augustin-Jean Fresnel, famous for his work in optics, born in 1788. A garden created on the marshy riverbank near the town centre displays willows, bamboo, ornamental rhubarb and other water-loving plants.

> ### *Did you know ?*
>
> *Prince Louis-Victor (1892–1987), seventh duke of Broglie, won the Nobel Prize for physics in 1929 after discovering that electrons had wavelike properties, so helping to lay the foundation of quantum mechanics.*

50C5

Choice of restaurants and bars (£–£££)

20 from Caen

3 a day from Lisieux in season

Dives-sur-Mer (▶ 64)

CABOURG ✪

This prosperous seaside resort has retained its 19th-century air of elegance. Dominating the long but featureless promenade is the Grand Hôtel, which lives up to its name and still trades on its association with Marcel Proust; the writer stayed here and based his fictional 'Balbec' on the town (▶ 104). The beach is long and sandy, overlooked by the Grand's wide windows that recall Proust's descriptions of passers-by gazing at the rich diners in their 'aquarium'.

Top right: *copper utensils in the kitchen of Carrouges*
Opposite: *enjoying the sun on Cabourg beach*

CANAPVILLE ✪

The bishops of Lisieux once resided here in the attractive timber-framed manor house set between the Touques river and the busy N177. Built between the 13th and 15th centuries, the Manoir des Évêques is set in attractive gardens and has interesting carvings – including one of a bishop's head on the gatepost.

🚹 51D5
🍽 Restaurants in village (£–££)
🚌 50/51 from Lisieux
🔄 Deauville (► 64), Pont l'Évêque (► 72), Trouville (► 75)

CARROUGES, CHÂTEAU DE ✪✪

An ornate stone gatehouse with four steep-roofed towers provides the entrance to this handsome red-brick building set in attractive parkland beyond the village of Carrouges. Until the 1930s the château was owned by the Le Veneur de Tillières family, who had lived there for nearly 500 years. The earliest part of the present building was built in the 14th century for Jean de Carrouges. Tours lead upstairs and downstairs: from the panelled Louis XI room, where the king himself stayed, to the 15th-century kitchen arrayed with pots and pans. A craft centre and the Parc Naturel Régional Normandie-Maine information centre are based in the park.

🚹 50C2
☎ 02 33 27 20 32
🕐 Mid-Jun to Aug, 9:30–11:30, 2–6; Apr to mid-Jun, Sep, 10–11:30, 2–5:30; Oct–Mar, 10–11:30, 2–4. Closed 1 Jan, 1 May, 1 Nov, 11 Nov, 25 Dec
🍽 La Boulangerie: teas and breakfasts for groups (££). In village, St-Pierre and Hôtel-Restaurant du Nord (£–££)
🚌 2 from Argentan/Alençon
♿ Few
💰 Expensive
🔄 Argentan (► 55), Sées (► 74)

50A4

☎ 02 33 57 34 63

🕐 Easter–Nov, 10–12, 2:30–6:30; Dec–Easter, Sun and public hols 2–6

🍴 Château de l'Abbaye hotel-restaurant (£££) near by

♿ Few

💰 Cheap

↔ Bayeux (► 18, 57), Château de Balleroy (► 57)

Above: *la Lande viaduct, crossing the Orne near Clécy*

51F4

☎ 02 32 34 84 34

🕐 May–Sep, daily 2–6; Mar–Nov, weekend and public hols 2–6

🍴 Restaurant (££)

🚌 24 from Évreux

💰 Moderate

50B3

🍴 Cafés and restaurants in town and on riverside (£–£££)

↔ Roche d'Oëtre (► 72), Thury-Harcourt (► 74)

CÉRISY-LA-FORÊT ✪

There has been a monastery in this quiet spot, on the edge of the Cérisy beech woods, since the 6th century. St Vigor established a community here about 510, and a later building was commissioned by William the Conqueror's father, Duke Robert. The present Benedictine abbey church dates from the 12th century, built in cream limestone and partly dismantled in 1812 when it proved too large for its new role of parish church. The west end of the nave has gone but the carved choir stalls in the apse have survived. Work continues to strengthen the transept where fissures have appeared; the foundations were previously reinforced in the 15th and 17th centuries. A small museum features statuary, floor tiles and other items rescued from the abbey church, and there is an exhibition of Romanesque art in lower Normandy.

CHAMP-DE-BATAILLE, CHÂTEAU DU ✪✪

This grand red-brick and stone château stands in a flat, open landscape ringed with woodland, and retains the atmosphere of an aristocratic country house. Part of the building is used as a golf club – the course is laid out within the grounds – but the main rooms are open to the public and include the duchess's bedroom, the billiard room, hung with tapestries, and a hall decorated with carvings representing the four seasons.

CLÉCY ✪

Houseboats, restaurants and bars line the Orne river on the approach to Clécy, which is centred on its 19th-century church. The main attraction of the village is its position in the Suisse Normande, surrounded by hill walks and viewpoints, one of the most popular being the Pain de Sucre that looks out across the Orne Valley. Model trains run around a miniature Suisse Normande at the Musée du Chemin de Fer Miniature (► 110).

CONCHES-EN-OUCHE ⭐

Conches lies on the edge of yet another ancient Norman territory, the Pays d'Ouche, with views of the Forêt de Conches to the west, and from the medieval château the lush Rouloir Valley to the east. The château ruins consist of a circular donjon and overgrown towers, all grouped on a motte and set in a small public garden. Near by, the Église Ste-Foy has an elaborate iron spire and carved 16th-century door. Both fortress and church are associated with the lords of Tosny: the former was built by them in the 12th century and the latter occupies the site of a church founded by Roger de Tosny in the 11th century, who returned from a pilgrimage bearing relics of Sainte Foy.

✚ 51F3
🍴 Choice of restaurants (£–££)
🚌 25 from Évreux
🚆 5 a day from Évreux
↔ Évreux (▶ 65)

CRÈVECŒUR-EN-AUGE ⭐⭐

An attractive cluster of traditional timber-framed and stone buildings represent the château founded here in the 11th century. Within the moated complex are remains of the donjon and its enclosure, and the chapel and workshops eventually taken over as farm buildings. These have been restored by the present owners, the Schlumberger Foundation, whose work in the oil industry is covered in an exhibition next door to the site.

✚ 51D4
☎ 02 31 63 02 45
🕐 Apr–Oct, daily 11–6 (Jul–Aug 11–7), Sun, Oct 2–6. Closed Tue in Apr, May, Jun, Sep
🍴 La Galetière (£–££)
🚌 52 from Lisieux during school terms
♿ Few
💰 Moderate
↔ Beuvron-en-Auge (▶ 59), Lisieux (▶ 66)

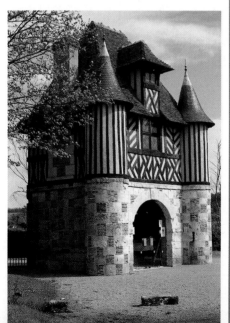

The 15th- to 16th-century gatehouse of the Château de Crèvecœur

51D5

Choice of restaurants and bars (££–£££)

20 from Caen, 51 from Le Havre

8 a day from Lisieux

Canapville (➤ 61), Trouville (➤ 75)

Above: *racing for the Grand Prix, Deauville*

50C5

Restaurants (£–££)

20 from Caen

3 a day from Lisieux in season

Cabourg (➤ 60)

50B2

Restaurants in new town (££)

4 from Argentan, or 34 from Caen to Flers, 5 from Flers

DEAUVILLE ✪✪

Two Côte Fleurie resorts, Deauville and Trouville, face each other across the Touques river – but it is Deauville that attracts the moneyed tourist. Eugène Cornuché built the racecourse, casino and les Planches, a long seafront boardwalk, in 1910, and each summer the big spenders continue to arrive; beach huts boast the names of celebrities past and present. From July to the end of August events include the American Film Festival, the Grand Prix horse race and a tennis tournament; out of season the town hibernates.

DIVES-SUR-MER ✪

Duke William embarked from this former inland port to conquer England, and later had a church built here, Notre-Dame, much restored and rebuilt since. Near by are the town's wooden *halles*, built in the 15th century so that the local monastery could collect market duties. Craft shops and a restaurant have been set up near the yachting marina in a 16th-century inn, now known as the Village Guillaume-le-Conquérant.

DOMFRONT ✪✪

Old and new Domfront sprawl from the ruined hilltop fortress high above the Varenne river. In the upper quarter, stone and timber-framed houses seem to grow from the ramparts and towers, and huddle for safety over narrow cobbled streets. The fortress was built in 1092 by the son of William the Conqueror, later King Henry I of England. On the riverside at the bottom of the hill is the 11th- to 12th-century Église Notre-Dame-sur-l'Eau, where Thomas à Becket is said to have celebrated mass in 1166.

ÉVREUX ●●

The ancient capital of Eure, on the banks of the Iton, has been rebuilt many times following invasion, siege and war, yet still preserves some notable historic monuments and an attractive centre. A riverside walk leads from the restored 12th- to 17th-century Cathédrale Notre-Dame to the Tour de l'Horloge, a free-standing tower built in 1490 whose bell strikes the hour.

Évreux's turbulent history is traced in the Musée de l'Ancien Évêché next to the cathedral, housed in the former 15th-century bishop's palace. Grouped around the central place Charles de Gaulle are the elegant 19th-century Hôtel Dieu, Maison des Arts, theatre, and the library with its startling modern annexe in the form of a wooden bowl. West of the centre lies the 12th-century Église St-Taurin; the one-time abbey church contains a fine 13th-century reliquary, gold-plated with enamelled silver, that contains the relics of Saint Taurin.

FALAISE ●●●

William the Conqueror's birthplace has become the subject of fierce controversy. It was at Falaise his father, Robert, took a fancy to Arlette, a tanner's daughter, as she washed her clothes in the river; rejecting all secrecy, she later met Robert inside the **château** and subsequently gave birth to William there. The modern controversy concerns the restoration of the site's 12th-century donjon, its chapel, and the 13th-century Tour de Talbot. Bruno Decaris's concrete and steel additions have shocked traditionalists, but their sudden plunging views and glimpses of thick stonework give a sense of the former military might often missing at similar monuments. A glass floor reveals the foundations of Duke Robert's stronghold, and delicately carved windows can be seen behind etched reinforced glass. A walk around the top of the Tour de Talbot offers dizzy views over the Ante Valley.

Above: *ornate craftsmanship on a fountain at Évreux*

ÉVREUX

➕ 51F4
🍴 Choice of restaurants (£–£££)
🚌 23 from Rouen, 24 from Honfleur
🚉 5 a day from Cherbourg
↔ Conches-en-Ouche (▶ 63)

FALAISE

➕ 50C3
🍴 La Fine Fourchette, rue G Clemenceau (£–££)
🚌 35 from Caen
↔ Château de Vendeuvre (▶ 75)

Château
☎ 02 31 41 61 44
🕐 Thu–Tue 10–6 (Sun 5). Closed late Dec to mid-Jan
♿ None
💷 Moderate
❓ Guided tours every hour; English tour 1:30

Left: *the mighty château at Falaise towers above the Ante river*

+ 50B5
☎ 02 31 80 00 42
⊙ Easter–Oct, Wed–Mon
2:30–6:30
🍴 Restaurant at Basly,
northeast, and in village
(££)
🚌 6 from Caen
✋ Expensive
↔ Caen (➤ 52–54)

FONTAINE-HENRY, CHÂTEAU DE ✪✪✪

As the D141 follows the Mue river towards Fontaine-Henry, the château can be glimpsed among the trees across the valley; but only when the road has climbed through the quiet Caen-stone hamlet is the building's extraordinary façade revealed. The earliest part, built in the 1490s for the Harcourt family, is a stone wing decorated with elegant carvings. The later wing, added in about 1550, is completely different: top-heavy with precipitous slate roofs that rise as high as the main walls below. Still privately owned, the château houses a collection of 17th-to 18th-century French paintings, and there is a late medieval chapel in the grounds.

+ 51D4
🍴 Choice of restaurants
(£–£££)
🚌 31 from Rouen
🚆 5 a day from Rouen,
10 a day from Évreux
(Paris–Dives line)
↔ Beuvron-en-Auge
(➤ 59), Crèvecœur-
en-Auge (➤ 63), Pont-
l'Évêque (➤ 72), St-
Germain-de-Livet
(➤ 72)

Les Buissonnets
✉ 22 Chemin des
Buissonnets
☎ 02 31 31 49 71
⊙ Easter–end Sep, daily
9–12, 2–6 (May and
Jun 5:30); Oct–Nov,
10–12, 2–5; Dec and
Feb–Easter, 10–12,
2–4. Closed Jan
♿ Few
✋ Free

LISIEUX ✪

Pilgrims come in thousands to Lisieux, the town where Sainte Thérèse lived as a child (➤ 67, panel). It is also the main centre of the Pays d'Auge. Apart from a scatter of old houses near the 13th-century cathedral and the Hôtel de Ville, the centre is largely modern and nondescript; the main interest lies in the places associated with Thérèse, including **les Buissonnets** where she lived as a girl. The massive, domed Basilique Ste-Thérèse, consecrated in the 1950s, stands out among concrete and glass office blocks; its 45m belfry houses no fewer than 44 bells, and an exhibition describes the life led by Thérèse and other Carmelite nuns. The saint's relics are kept in the Chapelle du Carmel, guarded by a statue of the Virgin that was once owned by her family.

Left: a statue of Sainte Thérèse, near les Buissonnets

Left: *a lavishly furnished bedroom in the Château de Fontaine-Henry*
Below: *the rooftops and greenery of Mortagne-au-Perche, once a regional capital, now a peaceful country town*

MORTAGNE-AU-PERCHE ✪✪

Former capital of the Perche, Mortagne stands on a hill overlooking a gentle landscape of meadows, red-roofed farms and wooded hills. Dilapidated houses with wrought-iron balconies line the streets, and the only remaining fortification, the Porte St-Denis, houses a regional museum, the Musée Percheron. The 15th-century Église Notre-Dame has good woodwork around the altar.

🚩 51E2
🍴 Choice of restaurants (£–££)
🚌 15 from Alençon
🔁 Alençon (► 55), Sées (► 74)

O, CHÂTEAU D' (► 20, TOP TEN)

ORBEC ✪✪

This unassuming market town has a good collection of crooked timber-framed houses, including the 16th-century Vieux Manoir that houses the **Musée Municipal**, whose collection of paintings, ceramics and other artefacts recall the history and traditions of the Pays d'Auge. The Église Notre-Dame has a massive belfry, originally a defensive tower in the 15th century but given a more decorative finish in the following century.

🚩 51E4
🍴 Restaurants in town (£–£££)
🚌 56 from Lisieux

Musée Municipal
✉ Grande Rue
☎ 02 31 61 12 35
🕐 Jun–Sep, daily 10–12:30, 2–5:30; May, Oct, daily 10–12, 2–6; Nov–Apr, weekend 10–12, 2–6
♿ None
🎫 Free
🔁 Broglie (► 60), Lisieux (► 66)

> ### *Did you know ?*
>
> *Sainte Thérèse was born Thérèse Martin in 1873. At the age of nine she begged her father to let her enter the Carmelite convent with her sister; she was admitted at 15, but died of tuberculosis at 24. Her pious memoirs,* History of a Soul, *were published posthumously, reaching a wide and enthusiastic readership. Thérèse was canonised in 1925 for her intense piety and devotion.*

67

In the Know

If you only have a short time to visit Normandy, or would like to get a real flavour of the region, here are some ideas:

10
Ways to Be a Local

Try your French – even a stumbling attempt will be much appreciated.

Relax in a café or brasserie with a coffee and a newspaper and let the world go by.

Forget about lunchtime shopping – many town and village shops in Normandy shut between 12 and 2 (but remain open long after office hours).

Visit an Algerian or Moroccan restaurant and try the cheap and tasty couscous or *tadjine* dishes.

Remember the courtesies of a language that still adheres to formality: always greet others with a *bonjour Madame* or *Monsieur*; take your leave with *au revoir* and the appropriate title.

Treat mealtimes as social occasions, a time for lively debate and discussion, not just for refuelling.

Use public transport – it's clean, efficient, and a great way to see the countryside.

See a film – the Normans (like the rest of France) are dedicated cinemagoers.

Learn to play *boules* – or, if that seems too daunting a task, linger to watch a quiet match in almost any village or corner of town.

Eat meat – or at least be prepared for the fact that vegetarian dishes are rarely even a token item on most restaurant menus.

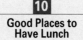

10
Good Places to Have Lunch

Auberge de Goury (£–££)
✉ Goury, Cap de la Hague ☎ 02 33 52 77 01. At the tip of the Cotentin peninsula, opposite a lifeboat station and lighthouse. Grills, seafood; closed Sunday evening and Monday evening.

Auberge St-Maclou (£–££)
✉ 224 rue Martainville, Rouen ☎ 02 35 71 06 67. Particularly good-value set menus at lunchtime in an old Rouen building near Église St-Maclou.

Camomille (££)
✉ 23 rue de Grenoble, Évreux ☎ 02 32 38 30 90. Generous omelettes and salads, and a good range of teas and pastries.

La Marine (£–££)
✉ 146 boulevard Fernand-Moureaux, Trouville ☎ 02 31 88 12 51. Fresh seafood in a traditional restaurant overlooking the fish market and river.

Le Pavé d'Auge (££–£££)
✉ place du Village, Beuvron-en-Auge ☎ 02 31 79 26 71. Norman dishes in the old market hall.

La Régence (££)
✉ 42 quai de Caligny, Cherbourg ☎ 02 33 43 05 16. Popular seafood restaurant (part of the Hôtel Régence), with good views of the harbour and fishing boats.

Les Roches Blanches (££)
✉ front de la mer, Étretat ☎ 02 35 27 07 34. Seafood with a fine sea view in a long building tucked under the cliff.

La Taverne de Maître Kanter (££) ✉ 1 avenue du 6 Juin, Caen ☎ 02 31 50 02 22. Brasserie serving salads, grills, sauerkrauts and seafood. Open midday to midnight.

Les Terrasses Poulard (£–££) ✉ 18 Grande Rue, le Mont-St-Michel ☎ 02 33 60 14 09. Omelettes and seafood on the mount, with spectacular bay views.

Le Vieux Honfleur (££–£££) ✉ 13 quai St-Étienne, Honfleur ☎ 02 31 89 15 31. Outdoor tables overlooking the harbour, with especially fine seafood.

Good fare and lively conversation in the resort of Honfleur

Children learning to sail at Le Havre

10
Top Activities

Canoeing on the Suisse Normande rivers, particularly the fast-flowing Orne.

Cycling along the Seine Valley, the Eure Valley and the Côte d'Albâtre; also in the forests of Brotonne and Lyons (▶ 115).

Fishing – sea fishing from resorts along the coast; also inland on lakes and rivers (▶ 114). Membership of angling associations and details of permits available at each *département* tourist office (▶ 120).

Golf – 27-hole courses open to amateurs at Deauville, Étretat and Granville; 18-hole courses at Cabourg, Caen, Clécy, Houlgate, Deauville, Dieppe, Évreux, Le Havre and Rouen (two); nine-hole courses at Bagnoles and Cherbourg (▶ 114).

Horse racing – courses at Alençon, Argentan, Caen, Deauville, Lisieux and Rouen, among many others.

Horse riding – treks and rides organised by centres throughout the region; along the shores of Calvados and Manche, and through woodlands and countryside in Eure and Orne (▶ 115).

Thalassotherapy (seawater therapy) along the Côte Fleurie, especially in Deauville, Luc-sur-Mer, Ouistreham and Trouville; also Dieppe and Granville.

Walking on footpaths along the Seine, between Étretat and le Tréport, and across the Parc Naturel Régional Normandie-Maine and the Cotentin peninsula. There are also steeper hikes in the Suisse Normande.

Windsurfing – good, long beaches on the coastline of Calvados and western Manche.

Yachting – marinas or moorings at Barfleur, Barneville-Carteret, Cabourg, Deauville, Dieppe, Granville, Fécamp, Le Havre, Honfleur, Ouistreham, St-Valéry-en-Caux, and le Tréport.

10
Top Views

• Seine Valley, from Château Gaillard (▶ 17).
• Rouvre Valley and Suisse Normande, from Roche d'Oëtre (▶ 72).
• Bay of le Mont-St-Michel, from the abbey (▶ 24–25).
• Vire Valley, from the Roches de Ham (▶ 90).
• The Baie d'Écalgrain and towards the Channel Islands, from Nez de Jobourg (▶ 82).
• Côte de Nacre, from the Pointe du Hoc (▶ 70).
• Côte d'Albâtre, from the Falaise d'Amont (▶ 39).
• Orne Valley, from Pain de Sucre, near Clécy (▶ 62).
• Hilltop spires of Coutances, on the northern approach (▶ 84).
• Remains of Abbaye de Hambye, in the Sienne Valley (▶ 85).

5
Conqueror Connections

• **Barfleur:** Duke William's flagship, *Mora*, shown on the Bayeux Tapestry, was built here.
• **Bayeux:** William's half-brother, Bishop Odo, completed the cathedral and commissioned the tapestry depicting William's victory at Hastings (▶ 18).
• **Caen:** William founded the two abbeys as mausoleums for himself and his wife (▶ 52).
• **Dives-sur-Mer:** William gathered his fleet and army here, prior to the invasion of England (▶ 64).
• **Falaise:** birthplace of William in 1027 (▶ 65).

🕂 50C5

🍴 Choice of cafés and restaurants near ferry terminal and beach (£–£££)

🚌 1 from Caen

↔ Caen (▶ 52–54), Cabourg (▶ 60)

🕂 51D3

☎ 02 33 36 68 68

🕐 Guided tour: Apr–Sep, daily 9:30–6; Oct–Mar, daily 2–4, Sun and public hols 9:30–5:30

🍴 Restaurant near by (££)

🚌 11 from Argentan to Nonant-le-Pin

♿ Moderate

🕂 50A5

🍴 Choice of restaurants at Grandcamp-Maisy

🚌 44; or 70 to Grandcamp-Maisy from Bayeux

One of the famous Percheron horses is put through its paces at le Pin-au-Haras

OUISTREHAM ✪

The ferry port of Ouistreham also offers a cheerful yacht marina and the beach resort of Riva-Bella. Set back from the coast, among suburban villas, are reminders of D-Day's Sword Beach: the Musée du Mur de l'Atlantique housed in the German range-finding station, Big Bunker; and the Musée du Débarquement No 4 Commando, opposite the casino, with military exhibits from World War II.

PIN-AU-HARAS, LE ✪✪

Louis XIV's minister Colbert set up the national stud in 1665, but it was abolished briefly during the Revolution. Re-established in the 19th century, its breeds include Percherons, Norman cobs and English thoroughbreds. Beyond the wrought-iron gate, topped with a gold horse's head, staff live and work in the 18th-century château, with the stable wings on either side. Walks and rides lead off into woodland, and the gentle Pays d'Auge landscape stretches into the distance.

POINTE DU HOC ✪✪✪

Nothing evokes the scale and violence of the 1944 landings more poignantly than this 30m clifftop position overlooking Omaha Beach. This German observation point was heavily bombarded, thus allowing American Rangers to climb the sheer rocks, albeit with heavy casualties; their story is told in the Musée des Rangers at Grandcamp-Maisy, 5km west. A viewing platform and memorial have been set up on the headland, a surreal landscape of modern megaliths: massive slabs of concrete lie scattered amid vast craters, now softened by grass. From the platform there are clear views of the invasion coast and the site itself, now silent except for the call of seagulls.

A Drive Along the D-Day Beaches

From Caen take the D514 towards Ouistreham.

A short detour (follow signs) leads to Pegasus Bridge, captured by British parachutists on 5 June 1944. Sound-and-light shows take place between April and October.

From Ouistreham (➤ 70) and Sword Beach, continue through St-Aubin and Courseulles (Juno Beach) to Arromanches (➤ 55).

Between Courseulles (with its colourful art-deco casino) and Arromanches, the flat marshes of the Gold Beach area offer wide sea views.

Follow the D514 from Arromanches and turn left on to the D127, joining the D87 before Ryes.

Continue through the village on the D87 to visit the British and Commonwealth cemetery.

From the cemetery return to the D112 and turn left, following signs to Sommervieu. Join the D12 into Bayeux (➤ 57). The D6 goes north to Port-en-Bessin and the Musée des Épaves sous-marines du Débarquement (Museum of Underwater Wrecks of the [D-Day] Landings). Follow the D514 along Omaha Beach.

At Colleville-sur-Mer, follow signs for the American cemetery, one of two war cemeteries for US troops.

Return to the D514 and continue west to Pointe du Hoc (➤ 70). Return to the D514 and turn right, continuing to Grandcamp-Maisy and the Musée des Rangers. The D199 goes south and joins the D113 (left) and D613 (left) for la Cambe and the German cemetery.

To continue to Utah Beach, take the N13 west, then the D913 to Ste-Marie-du-Mont, then drive to the coast.

Distance
80km to la Cambe; a further 28km to Utah Beach

Time
3½ hours to la Cambe without stops

Start point
Caen
🚪 50C4

End point
La Cambe
🚪 50A5

Lunch
Le Garde-Manger
(££)
✉ rue St-Jean, Bayeux
☎ 02 31 22 45 58

The first D-Day milestone, a 'Liberty Way' marker, at la Madeleine, near Utah Beach

➕ 51D5

🍴 Choice of restaurants
(£–£££)

🚌 50 from Lisieux

**Musée du Calvados et des
Métiers Anciens**

✉ Distillerie du Père
Magloire, route de
Deauville

☎ 02 31 64 12 87

🕐 Easter–Oct, 10–12:30,
2:30–6:30

💶 Cheap

➕ 50C3

🍴 Restaurant and bars at
Pont-d'Ouilly (£–££)

🚌 34 to Clécy from Caen

↔ Clécy (▶ 62)

Below: *the extraordinary
moated château at St-
Germain-de-Livet*

➕ 51D4

☎ 02 31 31 00 03

🕐 Apr–Sep,
Wed–Mon
10–11:30,
2–6:30;
Oct–Mar,
10–11:30,
2–4:30. Closed
early Oct,
Dec–Jan, 1
May

🍴 Restaurants at
Lisieux
(£–£££)

🚌 53 from
Lisieux

♿ Few

💶 Moderate

↔ Lisieux (▶ 66)

PONT-L'ÉVÊQUE ✪

Cheese is the principal claim to fame of this historic town in the Touques Valley. Its soft and creamy speciality was first produced in the 12th century, when it was known as Angelot; it only took the name of Pont-l'Évêque some 500 years later. Attractive timber-framed buildings survive, as well as the Flamboyant Église St-Michel where plaques commemorate the victims of the Franco-Prussian War and other conflicts. The **Musée du Calvados et des Métiers Anciens** describes traditional methods of making calvados. In the nearby Château de Bettevillethe, the Musée de la Belle Époque de l'Automobile has a collection of vintage vehicles (1800–1960s).

ROCHE D'OËTRE ✪✪

A track leads from the roadside to this 118m rocky precipice that offers some of the best views of the Suisse Normande's wooded slopes. A viewing table points out the main landmarks (take care – there's nothing between you and the drop): the panorama extends over the Orne Valley and the Rouvre gorges, and southeast towards the Lac du Rabodanges.

The small town of Pont-d'Ouilly, downriver, is a good centre for exploring the area, and has pleasant walks alongside the fast-flowing Orne.

ST-GERMAIN-DE-LIVET ✪✪✪

Hidden in the dip of an isolated tributary of the Touques is

a château straight from a children's picture book. The two surviving wings join at the ornate gatehouse: a 15th-century timber-framed range and a turreted 16th-century wing, its ostentatious chequered walls built using limestone, and green-glazed and red bricks. Frescos are preserved in the older house, while the later wing has a gallery of 19th-century paintings and a room decorated with terracotta tiles. The decorative style of brickwork found on the chateau can be seen also in the transept of the church opposite.

Antiques on sale in the St-Pierre halles

ST-PIERRE-SUR-DIVES ✪✪

On Monday mornings this small country town bursts into life as the market sets up in the cavernous, barn-like *halles*. Inside, the beamed roof echoes with the cacophony of ducks, turkeys, chickens and stall-holders, and the gabble continues at the brick stalls outside. Originally built in the 11th century, the hall was faithfully rebuilt after World War II using 290,000 wooden dowels and not a single nail. In the town's large church, once part of a Benedictine abbey, the 'Meridian', a line carved across the nave, flanked by signs of the zodiac and almost worn away in parts, indicates the position of the sun at noon.

SASSY, CHÂTEAU DE ✪

Beyond the hamlet of St-Christophe-le-Jajolet, on the brow of a wooded hill, this 18th-century red-brick château overlooks its terraced garden. It was begun in 1760 and passed in 1850 to the dukes of Audriffet-Pasquier, the current owners. Items on display include tapestries and a lock of hair cut from Louis XVI's head; the doomed king presented it to a member of the Pasquier family who had acted as his defence counsel.

🕂 51D4
🍽 Restaurants, cafés (£–££)
🚌 52 from Lisieux (during school terms)
🔄 Château de Vendeuvre (▶ 75)

Les Halles
🕐 Apr–Sep 8–8; otherwise apply to tourist office
🚹 Few
❓ Antiques market first Mon of every month

🕂 50C2
☎ 02 33 35 32 66
🕐 Easter–Oct, daily 3–6; grounds all year daily
🍽 None
🚌 12 from Alençon to St-Christophe-le-Jajolet
🎫 Moderate

73

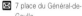

Above and right: *life on the beach and boardwalk at Trouville*

SÉES ⭐⭐

Sées, close to the source of the Orne on whose banks the town stands, has been an important religious centre since AD 400, when Saint Latuin became its first bishop. The town is dominated by its splendid Gothic cathedral, the classical bishop's palace, and the former canons' lodgings that now house the **Musée Départemental d'Art Religieux**. The western façade of the cathedral was bolstered with buttresses in the 16th century when it began to lean dangerously. Dramatic 13th-century stained-glass windows light the transept, and delicate tracery decorates the nave arcades and windows. In the porch, faded carvings can still be made out, including a cat carrying its kitten, and a double-headed eagle.

THURY-HARCOURT ⭐

This pleasant Suisse Normande centre, beside the Orne river, acquired its name from two sources: 'Thury', according to local legend, from a Viking cry, *Thor Aïe*; and Harcourt from the eponymous family who lived in the 11th-century château. Much of the former fortress was destroyed during World War II and only the skeletal façade remains, surrounded by restored gardens and a park.

TROUVILLE-SUR-MER ⊙⊙

Deauville's neighbour across the Touques estuary is the more appealing and cheerful of the two resorts, with its fishing boats along the quayside, the tree-lined boulevard Fernand Moureaux, and a wide sandy beach and boardwalk. Garish lights advertise the Louisiana Follies at the salmon-pink casino, and fish, reptiles and insects are on display at the Aquarium Écologique. Set back from the seafront, the Église Notre-Dame de Bon-Secours has intricate stained-glass windows and an ornate 19th-century façade, and the Musée Villa Montebello houses paintings by Eugène Boudin; the museum also traces the history of sea bathing that became the rage here in the 1820s.

➕ 51D5
🍴 Choice of restaurants along boulevard Fernand Moureaux and rue Carnot (£–££)
🚌 51 from Lisieux, 20 from Caen
🚂 8 a day from Lisieux
🔁 Canapville (▶ 61), Deauville (▶ 64)

VENDEUVRE, CHÂTEAU DE ⊙⊙

Set among formal flower beds and an ornamental water garden, this 18th-century château houses some intriguing curiosities, including a chair designed for fashion-conscious women in panniers (the 'saddlebags' worn to widen skirts). The main attraction, though, is the Musée de Mobilier Miniature, a collection of tiny masterpieces made from the 16th century to the present day. These include silverware, embroidery, furniture and cutlery, all in immaculate scaled-down detail; one of the most popular items is a miniature bed, complete with hangings, made in the 18th century for the pet cat of Louis XV's daughter.

➕ 50C4
☎ 02 31 40 93 83
🕐 May–Sep, daily 10–6; Mar–Apr, Oct to mid-Nov, weekend and public hols 2–6; or by appointment
🍴 Tea room (££)
♿ Few
💰 Expensive
🔁 Falaise (▶ 65), St-Pierre-sur-Dives (▶ 73)

VERNEUIL-SUR-AVRE ⊙

Historic Verneuil is composed of three precincts, each once protected by a series of moated walls, and you can still walk along part of the outer moat that enclosed the whole town. The grim, windowless Tour Grise was built by Philippe Auguste after the French had taken the town in 1204, a circular donjon similar to the Tour Jeanne d'Arc in Rouen (▶ 35). The town further suffered during the Hundred Years War due to its position on the border between French and English territory. Timber-framed and stone buildings crowd around the Église de la Madeleine, a 12th-century church whose later, Flamboyant tower is crowned with an elegant filigree lantern. The Église Notre-Dame has 16th-century statuary by local sculptors.

➕ 51F3
🍴 Restaurants and bars in town (£–£££)
🚌 26 from Évreux

The richly carved late 15th-century tower of la Madeleine, Verneuil-sur-Avre

Food & Drink

Weight-watchers are in for a tough time in Normandy. Rich dairy ingredients, mountains of fresh seafood, and local cider are just some of the temptations in store.

Pommeau

Given the abundance of local orchards it's not surprising that apples appear so frequently – on meat, in puddings and in drinks. *Pommeau* is yet another ingenious way of using the fruit: a combination of two parts apple juice and one part calvados, chilled and served as an aperitif. It can also be used, with added spices, as an ingredient in savoury dishes.

Dairy Products

Normandy boasts some of the country's most delicious and best-known cheeses. Pont-l'Évêque, a soft and creamy cheese, is made with fresh warm milk and sold in squares. The stronger and smellier Livarot, made from staler milk, is round and banded with 'stripes' that earn it the nickname 'le colonel'. Neufchâtel is a cream cheese packaged in a variety of shapes and edible after 12 days (but better after several months). Heading the bill, though, is Camembert, now made in thousands of different versions in many corners of Europe. Normandy Camembert is the genuine article: the very best bears the letters VCN (*véritable Camembert de Normandie*). Because of the wealth of dairy farms, Normans have a passion for cream and butter, particularly in the rural Pays d'Auge where almost any dish – fish, meat, potatoes or vegetables – can be served with a dairy sauce *à la vallée d'Auge*.

A variety of Camemberts – but only Normandy's version is the real thing

Seafood

Some of the freshest and tastiest seafood you will ever sample is served up in the harbourside restaurants of the coastal resorts. The list is mouthwatering: lobsters, mussels, oysters, crabs, and a multitude of fish. *Marmite dieppoise* combines the best of all worlds: a spicy stew with shrimp, mussels and white fish; for an even more impressive concoction order an *assiette de fruits de mer*, a mixture of mussels, oysters, clams, cockles, crabs and more. The pick of the seafood eateries can be found along the quays of Dieppe, Honfleur and Granville.

Meat and Offal

Squeamish carnivores would do well to avoid asking too many questions about the local menus – especially in Rouen, where the main ingredient of *canard* (duck) *rouennais* is put through all sorts of agonies for the gourmet's benefit. In order to keep the full flavour of its blood, the unfortunate bird is either strangled or smothered; alternatively it is squeezed through a press so that the juice of its bones gives an added edge to the sauce. Thus vegetarianism is a lonely occupation in a region where menus include Mortagne-au-Perche's famous *boudin noir* (black pudding), Vire's *andouilles* (chitterlings), and *tripes à la mode de Caen*, which is served after stewing for several hours.

L'Andouille de Vire

Vire chitterlings have been a local speciality since the 18th century. The sausages, made from the pig's digestive system, are smoked for six to eight weeks before being steeped and cooked in water for three or four hours. Two factors apparently account for the success of Vire's *andouille*: the cleanliness of the offal, and the long smoking process that gives it a particularly robust flavour.

Desserts and Drinks

Apples and pears feature prominently in Norman puddings, as well as in the most celebrated drinks, cider and calvados. Calvados, named after the *département*, is a brandy made from fermented and distilled apples matured in oak for up to 10 years. The *trou* (hole) *normand* is the custom of knocking back a small glass of calvados in the middle of a meal to stimulate the digestion. (Nowadays it's more likely to be a calvados and apple sorbet.) Perry, or *poiré*, is made from pears in the same way cider is produced from apples.

Popular desserts are *douillon* (pear baked in pastry) and *bouillon* (a kind of apple dumpling).

Above and below: *making the best of apples and pears in* tarte Normande; Pommeau, poiré *and cider*

The Northwest

As you cross the border into Manche and travel towards the head of the Cotentin (Cherbourg) peninsula, the landscape changes and the population dwindles. At the base of the Cotentin are the fields and orchards of the *bocage*, criss-crossed with dense hedges. Empty beaches and sand dunes line the western coast, and at the tip of the peninsula waves crash against wild, granite cliffs. Cherbourg is the biggest centre, with its constant stream of ferry passengers and busy port, but the most memorable sight in the northwest – indeed in the whole of Normandy – is le Mont-St-Michel (▶ 24–25), perched upon the quicksands in the crook between Normandy and Brittany.

> ' *Mont–St–Michel, said Victor Hugo, is to France what the pyramids are to Egypt. This does not describe it; but then it is indescribable …* '

PERCY DEARMER
Highways and Byways in Normandy
(1900)

——————●——————

Opposite: *memories of le Mont-St-Michel*

NORTHWEST NORMANDY

0   10   20 km

6

Cap de la Hague · Goury
Auderville
Baie d'Ecalgrain
Nez de Jobourg · Beaumont
Cap Lévy
Pointe de Barfleur
Querqueville · Tourlaville · Maupertus-sur-Mer · Barfleur
Vauville · **Cherbourg**
Château de Tourlaville · Quettehou
5
Martinvast · St-Vaast-la-Hougue
les Pieux · Quinéville
Valognes
Bricquebec · Montebourg
C o t e n t i n · **Utah Beach**
Carteret · Barneville-Carteret · St-Saveur-le-Vicomte · Ste-Mère-Église · Grandcamp-Maisy
Cap de Carteret
4
Portbail · Ste-Marie-du-Mont
St-Jorès · Isigny-sur-Mer
JERSEY
(GBJ) · la-Haye-du-Puit · **Carentan**
St-Germain-Plage
Lessay
Tante
Vire
Château de Pirou · Périers
3
Château de Gratot · **St-Lô**
Coutainville · **Coutances** · Torigni-sur-Vire
Agon-Coutainville · **Roches de Ham**
Hauteville-Plage
Tessy-sur-Vire
Sienne
Abbaye de Hambye
Bréhal · Gavray · Pont-Farcy
Percy
Villedieu-les-Poêles · St-Sever-Calvados
2
Granville · **Abbaye de la Lucerne**
Baie du Mont-St-Michel
Jullouville · Sartilly · Brécey
Carolles
Pointe du Grouin · St-Jean-le-Thomas · Sourdeval
Rothéneuf
Cancale · **Avranches** · **L'Abbaye Blanche**
St-Malo · le Mont-St-Michel · Pontaubault · Mortain
Ducey
1
Sélune · St-Hilaire-du-Harcouët
Dol-de-Bretagne · Pontorson
St-James
A · **B** · **C**

What to See in the Northwest

AVRANCHES ✪✪

The hilltop town above the Sée river looks out across the estuary to the church of le Mont-St-Michel, originally founded in the 8th century by Bishop Aubert of Avranches after Saint Michael had appeared to him in a vision. **Les Manuscrits du Mont-St-Michel** in the Hôtel de Ville are a collection of illuminated manuscripts associated with the famous abbey, including some fine Romanesque drawings. Behind the building are remains of an 11th-century château; steps climb to the donjon and terraced garden, with views inland and over the coast. The 19th-century Église de Notre-Dame-des-Champs is one of three churches built after the old cathedral collapsed in 1790.

🚹 80B1
🍴 Choice of restaurants (£–££)
🚌 31 from Cherbourg, 31 from Granville
🚉 2 a day from Caen

Les Manuscrits du Mont-St-Michel
☎ 02 33 89 29 49
🕐 Jul–Aug, daily 10–6; Jun–Sep daily 10–12, 2–6
💶 Cheap

BARFLEUR ✪✪

Fishing boats chug in and out, and fishermen mend their nets on the harbourside of this small granite town on the Cotentin's northeast tip. It was near here that William 'Atheling', son of King Henry I, was drowned when the White Ship sank in 1120 – an event that later led to a civil war over the English crown. A narrow passageway runs from the harbour past the 17th-century church to a beach and Normandy's tallest lighthouse (71m).

🚹 80C5
🍴 Some cafés and bars in town (£–££)
🚌 1 from Cherbourg
⛴ St-Vaast-la-Hougue (▶ 88)

Barfleur, a traditional fishing town

BARNEVILLE-CARTERET ✪

Barneville-Carteret is a union of two different towns and their beaches. Carteret is the busier resort, with a yachting marina, and a broad sandy beach overlooked by caravans and large faded villas. Ferries travel from the harbour to Jersey and Guernsey.

Barneville, 2km away, has an austere 11th-century church with a fortified tower added later. Barneville-Plage, a long, empty stretch of sand, is reached across a cob over the Gerfleur estuary.

🚹 80A4
🍴 Restaurants in Barneville and by Carteret beach (£–£££)
🚌 3 from Cherbourg
⛴ Bricquebec (▶ 82)

80B4

🍴 Vieux Château
(incorporated into castle);
cafés and bars in town
(£–££)

🚌 4 from Cherbourg

↔ Barneville-Carteret
(► 81), Valognes (► 88)

BRICQUEBEC ✪

The impressive ruins of a 14th-century château form the focus of this small market town, whose main street runs right up to the gatehouse. Inside, the 11-sided donjon is the most prominent of a group of buildings around a pleasant courtyard; one side is taken up with the older Knights' Hall, now the Hôtel du Vieux Château. A walk along the sentry wall leads to the clock tower that houses a collection of traditional Norman furniture.

80A5

🍴 Auberge de Goury, near
Goury lifeboat station
(£–££); *crêperie* and
Auberge des Grottes in
high season at Nez de
Jobourg car park (£);
restaurants and bars at
Auderville (£–££)

↔ Cherbourg (► 83)

CAP DE LA HAGUE ✪✪✪

Heading west from Cherbourg, the road to the north-western finger of the Cotentin passes the vast, glittering pile of the Usine de Retraitement des Combustibles Nucléaires (nuclear fuel reprocessing centre), then turns left, between high hedges and through the narrow, dark-stone village of Dannery, for the wild rocky headland at Nez de Jobourg. A track leads past an isolated *auberge* to a viewpoint that looks across the coastline and green fields (marred only by the nuclear plant in the distance), and out to sea towards the Channel Islands. From Dannery the road winds north through a green valley to emerge at the Baie d'Écalgrain, a lovely sweep of coast sheltered by low hills. Beyond the village of Auderville the road comes to an end at Goury, a tiny harbour with a lighthouse and hexagonal lifeboat station; here you can enjoy a meal and watch the waves from the quayside.

80B2

🍴 Cafés and bars at
Jullouville 4km north of
Carolles, on D911 (£);
snack bars and restaurant
at Carolles-Plage (£); bar
and *crêperie* in
Carolles (£)

🚌 29 from Granville

↔ Avranches (► 81),
Granville (► 85)

CAROLLES ✪

Carolles is a quiet coastal village with an unassuming beach resort, set between the bustling holiday centre of Granville and Avranches. The location is its main appeal: walks lead from the centre through wooded countryside

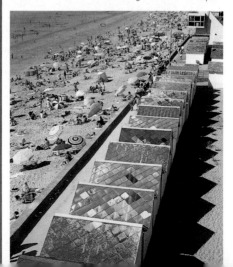

Beach huts add colour to the resort of Carolles

and along the Vallée du Lude to a remote bay. Carolles-Plage, a stretch of sand backed with beach huts and snack bars, looks north along the spectacular coastline as far as Granville. A viewpoint to the northwest, le Pignon Butor, takes in the Baie du Mont-St-Michel between Granville and the Breton headland of Pointe du Grouin.

CHERBOURG ●●

Ships have docked here since the 17th century when Vauban built the original port, and today a constant stream of ferries sail to and from England and Ireland. But the town has a life of its own, too, with theatre and restaurants grouped around the place Général de Gaulle, a pleasant pedestrianised shopping centre, and hotels and cafés overlooking the port and fishing boats. Paintings displayed in the Musée Thomas-Henry, behind the port, include work by Fra Filippo Lippi and Fra Angelico. An eclectic collection in the **Musée d'Ethnographie**, set in tropical gardens, illustrates cultures and societies from around the world, including the life of the Inuit (Eskimo). Above the town, Fort du Roule, the scene of fierce fighting in 1944, houses a museum about the war years.

In Tourlaville, 5km southeast of Cherbourg, a château with an elegant façade and attractive grounds (open all year) was the setting for a 16th-century sex scandal, when Julien and Marguerite Ravalet, children of the owners, ran off together and lived as lovers until they were convicted of incest and executed in 1603.

Work and play – fishing boats and yachts share part of the busy harbour at Cherbourg

➕ 80B5
🍴 Choice of restaurants along quai de Caligny (£–££)
🚌 1 from St-Lô
🚂 7 a day from Évreux and Caen (on line from Paris St Lazare)
↔ Cap de la Hague (► 82)

Musée d'Ethnographie
✉ parc E Liais
☎ 02 33 53 51 61
🕐 All year, Tue–Sat 10–12, 2–5 (Jul–Aug till 6); Sun 2–5. Closed public hols
♿ Few
💷 Cheap

80B3

 Choice of restaurants and cafés (£–££)

1 from Cherbourg

Château de Gratot (▶ 85)

Musée Quesnel-Morinière

✉ 2 rue Quesnel-Morinière

☎ 02 33 45 11 92

🕐 Daily except Tue and Sun morning. Jul–Aug 10–12, 2–6; Jan–Jun and Sep–Dec 10–12, 2–5 Closed public hols

♿ None

 Cheap

Above: *the hilltop spires of Coutances*

COUTANCES ✪✪✪

The Gothic spires of the cathedral soar above the town on its outcrop overlooking the Soulles river. The present church, completed in 1274 with two graceful 80m steeples and a 57m octagonal lantern tower, replaced the Romanesque cathedral built by Bishop Geoffroy de Montbray in the mid-11th century. Inside, the eye is drawn upwards by the tall arcades, past lancet windows and stained glass to the vault, while light pours in through the side-chapel windows. The life of Thomas à Becket and the Day of Judgement are depicted in the magnificent transept windows.

Coutances is a peaceful and prosperous town, with public gardens laid out on the hillside above the Bulsard tributary and the three remaining arches of its 14th-century aqueduct. The 17th-century Hôtel Poupinel at the garden's entrance houses the **Musée Quesnel-Morinière**, with a fine collection of paintings, furniture and dress.

GRANVILLE ⭐⭐

Granville is a town with a many-sided character. There's the busy port with its lively fishing fleet, a terminal for ferries to the Channel Islands, and then there is the boisterous summer resort with shops, restaurants, and the modern Aquarium du Roc that houses a 'shell wonderland' and butterfly garden (▶ 111).

On the narrow headland above the modern town lies the Haute Ville, entered through a grim gateway (Grande Porte) complete with chained drawbridge. The upper town's ramparts were built by the English in the 15th century; within, houses huddle along the grid of streets that leads to the granite Église Notre-Dame and, behind it, former barracks. Stone steps just inside the Grande Porte climb up to the **Musée du Vieux Granville** that contains artefacts illustrating the history of the port.

Beyond the walls, the lighthouse on the Pointe du Roc offers good views; northeast, Christian Dior's childhood home has changing exhibits about the designer.

Boats travel to the nearby Îles Chausey, once quarried for granite. Just under 2km long, Grande Île is large enough for a small hotel, a 19th-century fort built against British attack, and a lighthouse.

GRATOT, CHÂTEAU DE ⭐⭐

Hidden behind a church in quiet farmland are the remains of this château built between the 14th and 18th centuries. The site was later used as farm buildings until renovation by volunteers in the 1960s. A roofless main hall, with a fireplace, is flanked by two towers, one of which – the octagonal Tour à la Fée (Fairy Tower) – is decorated with carved foliage and gargoyles, and topped with a delicate stone trellis. Behind the hall, an arched bridge leads across the moat and steps climb to an empty field, once formal gardens. The château was the home of the Argouges family, and an exhibition in the outbuildings tells their story, including an artist's impression of the gardens in their former glory.

HAMBYE, ABBAYE DE ⭐

Founded in 1145 by Guillaume Paynel, the Abbaye de Hambye is now a fragile ruin in the tranquil valley of the Sienne. The transept tower survives intact and appears to balance precariously on delicate arches; flying buttresses and the nave's high lancet windows add to the impression that the whole structure could be blown away on the wind. Outbuildings house Rouen tapestries, sculptures, frescos, and paintings of the abbey.

GRANVILLE

➕ 80B2
🍴 Choice of restaurants on harbourside (£–£££)
🚢 1 from Cherbourg
🚆 4 a day from Argentan (Paris Montparnasse line)
🔄 Carolles (▶ 82), Abbaye de la Lucerne (▶ 86)

Musée du Vieux Granville

✉ 2 rue Lecarpentier
☎ 02 33 50 44 10
🕐 Apr–Jun, Wed–Sun 10–12, 2–6; Jul–Sep, Wed–Mon 10–12, 2–6; Oct–Mar, Wed and weekend 2–6
♿ None
💰 Cheap

GRATOT, CHÂTEAU DE

➕ 80B3
☎ 02 31 27 97 40
🕐 All year daily 10–12:45, 2–7
🍴 Le Tourne-Bride (££), between Gratot and Coutances, on D44
♿ Few
💰 Moderate (pay at coin box in gatehouse)
🔄 Coutances (▶ 84)

HAMBYE, ABBAYE DE

➕ 80C2
☎ 02 33 61 76 92
🕐 Guided tours: Feb to mid-Dec, 10–12, 2–6. Closed Tue in winter
🍴 Auberge de l'Abbaye (££–£££), on D51 near by
💰 Moderate

➕ 80B3
🍴 Limited choice in town
(£); or southeast on D900
and south on D57 to le
Mesnilbus, Auberge des
Bonnes Gens (£–£££)
🚌 1 from Cherbourg
↔ Château de Pirou (➤ 87)

*Above: the east apse of
the abbey church, Lessay*

➕ 80B2
☎ 02 33 48 83 56
🕐 Feb–Dec, 9–12, 2–6:30.
Closed Tue Feb–Mar
🍴 Auberge near by (££); or
west on D973 at St-
Pierre-Langers, Le Jardin
de l'Abbaye (££–£££)
♿ None
⬛ Moderate
↔ Granville (➤ 85)

LESSAY ★★

Lessay's abbey, Ste-Trinité, was founded in 1056 by
Turstin Haldup, lord of la Haye-du-Puits to the north, and
completed early in the 12th century. The ancillary monastic
buildings suffered in the Hundred Years and Religious
wars, and, having been completely rebuilt in the 18th
century, were destroyed in 1944. The restored church,
however, survives as a fine example of Romanesque architecture, with glowing limestone walls and roof tiles
covered in golden lichen. There are three tiers to the nave,
with a gallery connecting the uppermost windows.
Subdued stained glass adds to the simple tranquillity.

LUCERNE, ABBAYE DE ★

Since 1959 the ruins of this 12th-century abbey in the
isolated Thar Valley have undergone gradual restoration.
The monastic church, used for concerts in the summer,
has a Romanesque doorway and an elaborate 18th-century
organ. There are also remains of a 19th-century aqueduct,
built for a mill in the grounds, along with the tithe barn,
abbot's house and dovecote. An arcaded Romanesque
lavatorium – a monastic washstand – survives near the old
refectory. Sunday mass is still held in the church.

LE MONT-ST-MICHEL (➤ 24–25, TOP TEN)

MORTAIN ✪

Mortain occupies a high ridge overlooking the steep Sélune Valley and Forêt de Mortain. The stark bell tower of **Église St-Évroult** rises above the main street; inside, the church treasury houses an 8th-century casket, the Chrismale, a reliquary decorated with angels and runic script, probably made in one of the English kingdoms. North of the centre, the buildings of the 12th-century Abbaye Blanche are actually dark and stern, despite the name. A walk from the abbey leads to two waterfalls – the Grande and Petite Cascade.

🚩 80C1
🍴 Bars and restaurants in town (£–££)
🔁 Vire (▶ 89)

Église St-Évroult
☎ 02 33 59 19 74
🕐 Jul–Aug, Tue, Thu, Sat 3–4; otherwise apply to tourist office
♿ None
💷 Free

The Romanesque cloister arcade at the Abbaye Blanche, Mortain

PIROU, CHÂTEAU DE ✪✪

A gatehouse and castellated walkway lead to substantial ruins in remote farmland near the dunes of the western Cotentin. Ramparts protect the various medieval buildings, stacked up on a moated bailey, including the chapel, bakehouse, kitchens and guardroom; a modern tapestry in the knights' hall relates the Norman conquest of southern Italy and Sicily.

🚩 80B3
☎ 02 33 46 34 71
🕐 Daily 9–12, 2–6:30. Closed Tue in winter
🍴 Bar (£) in Pirou; restaurant on road near by (£)
💷 Moderate

ST-LÔ ✪

Following the bombardment of 1944 that destroyed most of its buildings St-Lô has been rebuilt as a modern town, but with a distinct character of its own. The old town walls survive in part and a single tower guards one corner of the central place Général-de-Gaulle. Market stalls set up under the roof of the tourist office; the office itself allows access to a modern tower giving views over the Vire Valley. The west front of the Église Notre-Dame has been left in its bomb-damaged state, the modern bronze doors a telling contrast to the battered 13th- to 17th-century façade; within, photographs show the extent of the wartime devastation. The Musée des Beaux Arts in the Centre Culturel Jean Lurçat has a collection of paintings and 16th-century tapestries.

🚩 80C3
🍴 Choice of restaurants and bars (£–££)
🚌 1 from Cherbourg
🚌 2 a day from Caen

> ### *Did you know ?*
>
> *When the White Ship went down off Barfleur in 1120, it took with it William 'Atheling', son of Henry I of England, signalling the end of the Norman dynasty. Every year, through the night of 24–25 November, the bell at Lucerne tolls in mourning.*

ST-VAAST-LA-HOUGUE ✪✪

Cafés overlook the harbour of this cheerful seaside town, famous for its oysters, where yachts and fishing boats jostle for space. Silhouetted at the tip of the southern causeway is Vauban's Fort de la Hougue. At the far end of a wharf is the Chapelle des Marins, a simple stone seamen's chapel with geometric carvings over the doorway. A bird sanctuary and the Musée Maritime of Tatihou Island lie across a narrow channel.

STE-MÈRE-ÉGLISE ✪

In a modern building near the market place, the Musée des Troupes Aéroportées commemorates the night of 5 June 1944 when paratroops were dropped over Ste-Mère-Église to support the American army. Among them was Private John Steel, whose parachute became entangled on the church steeple; he hung there for two hours until rescued by German soldiers. Each summer a dummy parachutist is suspended from the steeple. A 16th-century farm on the edge of town, the Ferme-Musée du Cotentin, has displays about local rural life.

VALOGNES ✪✪

The modern centre of Valognes, built after the war, is unremarkable, but the older quarter beyond has real charm. Mellow stone houses back on to a stream crossed by footbridges; one of them, the 15th-century Logis du Grand Quartier, houses the Musée Régional du Cidre et du Calvados that tells the story of cider-making. Fragments of Roman buildings stand in a pleasant garden, and some grand 17th- to 18th-century houses survive, including the Hôtel de Granval-Caligny, home of 19th-century writer Jules Barbey d'Aurevilly, and the Hôtel de Beaumont, a graceful building with formal gardens.

🔲 80C5
🍴 Choice of restaurants, especially near harbour (£–££). Hôtel de France et des Fuchsias, 20 rue Maréchal-Foch (£–££)
🚌 1 from Cherbourg
↔️ Barfleur (➤ 81), Valognes (➤ 88)

🔲 80C4
🍴 Some restaurants and cafés in town (£–££)
🚌 Buses from Cherbourg marked 'Ste-Mère-Église'

🔲 80B5
🍴 Choice of hotel-restaurants in centre (£–£££)
🚌 1, 4 from Cherbourg
🚆 6 a day from Cherbourg (Paris St-Lazare line)
↔️ Bricquebec (➤ 82), Cherbourg (➤ 83), St-Vaast-la-Hougue (➤ 88), Ste-Mère-Église (➤ 88)

Polished work by a coppersmith in Villedieu-les-Poëles

VILLEDIEU-LES-POËLES ✪✪

Copper pots and tin pans fill the shop windows of Villedieu's long main street (*poêles* means 'pans'). This has been a metalworking centre since the 12th century when the Knights Hospitallers (later 'of Malta') were established in the town. An alley leads from the main street between dark granite houses to the Maison de l'Étain (House of Pewter), while opposite is the Atelier du Cuivre (copper workshop). Bells are still cast in the **Fonderie de Cloches**, set on an island in the Sienne. There are yet more attractions crowded into the little town: a lace-making museum; a clockmaker's workshop; and the Maison du Meuble Normand, across the Sienne behind the main street, with a collection of traditional Norman furniture.

VIRE ✪

This major route junction in a bend of the Vire river is visited by an endless stream of traffic. At place 6 Juin 1944 cars besiege the 13th-century gate and belfry, the **Porte-Horloge**. There are few other survivors of the historic town devastated in World War II: among shops south of the gateway are two defensive towers, and on an eminence above the river are remains of a 12th-century donjon. Local traditions are recalled in the Musée de Vire, set in the quiet cobbled courtyard of the Hôtel-Dieu.

Textile mills once dotted the surrounding *bocage* . Here during the 15th century, in the district known as Vaux de Vire, Olivier Basselin penned his popular poems and songs, the precursors of vaudeville.

Left: a *reminder of World War II in the Musée des Troupes Aéroportées, Ste-Mère Église*

✚ 80C2
🍴 Restaurants, bars (£–££)
🚌 4 a day from Granville/Argentan/Vire (Paris Montparnasse line)
🔁 Abbaye de Hambye (▶ 85)

Fonderie de Cloches

✉ Atelier Cornille Harvard, 10 rue du Pont Chignon
☎ 02 33 61 00 56
🕐 Tue–Sat 8–12, 1:30–5:30 (mid-Jun to mid-Sep, daily)
💵 Moderate

✚ 50A3
🍴 Choice of restaurants and cafés (£–£££)
🚌 25 or Bus Vert 32 from Caen
🚌 4 a day from Granville/Argentan (Paris Montparnasse line)
🔁 Mortain (▶ 87)

Porte-Horloge

✉ place du 6 Juin 1944
☎ 02 31 68 00 05 (tourist office)
🕐 Jul to mid-Sep, Mon–Sat 2:30–6:30
💵 Cheap

A Drive Through the Vallée de la Vire

Distance
75km

Time
About 2½ hours without stops

Start point
St-Lô
 50A4

End point
Vire
 50A3

Lunch
Auberge de la Chapelle (£)
✉ Troisgots, north of la-Chapelle-sur-Vire
☎ 02 33 56 32 83

This route winds up and down the green Vire Valley, through peaceful *bocage* countryside.

Take the N174 from St-Lô (➤ 87) to Torigni-sur-Vire.

This fast road sweeps through wooded, rolling farmland to Torigni, a small town with a camping site and lakes, where the Château des Matignon has a display of 17th- and 18th-century tapestries and sculptures.

At the junction by the château, turn right (Tessy-sur-Vire). Cross the roundabout and turn right just before the water tower; then follow signs left, through Brectouville, and right to Roches de Ham.

The road climbs gradually past farms and orchards to this spectacular 80m viewpoint looking down over the curving river and its valley.

Return down the D551 to a right turn (D396), crossing the Vire and climbing the other side of the valley. Turn left to Troisgots and la-Chapelle-sur-Vire.

Pilgrims still come to la Chapelle's riverside church to see its 15th-century statue of Our Lady of Vire; on the opposite bank an ornate gateway and steps lead to the Stations of the Cross.

Turn left with the D159/D359, crossing the river again. At a junction, turn right to Tessy-sur-Vire. Then take the D374/D21 (signed Vire) through Pont-Farcy, and turn left (D307) to Ste-Marie-Outre-l'Eau. The road swings left round the church. Follow the D307 past the Pont-Bellenger turning for the D185 to Campeaux. Join the N174 (right, to Vire), then turn left (D293) and follow the river to the D56 (right) and le Bény-Bocage.

There are good views of the upper Vire Valley from this attractive town, and several viewpoints near by.

After leaving le Bény-Bocage turn right (D577) and continue to Vire (➤ 89).

Where To...

- Tarte d'Yport
- Nid d'Abeilles
- Gâteau Basque
- Beignet Framboise
- Chaquettes
- Crepes
- Pain Bagnat
- Pain Briard
- Tourte "Maupassant"
- Nouillette
- Pain Brioché

Above: *a colourful display of
Camembert cheese labels*
Right: *treats on offer from the
local boulanger*

Rouen

Prices

Ratings are based on a three-course meal for one, without wine:

£ = up to €15 (F100)

££ = €15–38 (F100–250)

£££ = over €38 (F250)

Fast Food

The rue des Carmes is a lively Rouen street of shops, hotels and quick-and-cheap eateries. Try the self-service restaurant Funch, at No 60 (☎ 02 35 71 81 81), or Pizza Paï above it, one of a popular French chain of pizzerias (☎ 02 35 07 73 94).

Auberge St-Maclou (£–££)

A range of set menus offers traditional Norman food served in a beamed dining-room. Quiet location in an old building near Église St-Maclou.

✉ 224 rue Maratainville ☎ 02 35 71 06 67 🕐 Lunch, dinner

L'Auberge du Vieux Carré (££–£££)

This old-fashioned and intimate restaurant is tucked away off one of the old town's shopping streets. Muted conversation and familiar – though beautifully prepared – dishes. In fine weather the tables are set in a sheltered courtyard; inside, the dining-room is furnished with antiques and paintings.

✉ 34 rue Ganterie ☎ 02 35 71 67 70 🕐 Lunch, dinner. Closed early Aug

Le Beffroy (££–£££)

Straightforward local cooking using cider; good seafood and a reliable choice of game. The setting is a very old building in a quiet street; the atmosphere is smart but animated. A popular choice.

✉ 15 rue Beffroy ☎ 02 35 71 55 27 🕐 Lunch, dinner. Closed Tue and Sun eve

La Cave Royale (££)

North African specialities served in an atmospheric setting, with colourful pots, scarves and rugs providing decoration around the candlelit tables. For healthy appetites, try the gargantuan Tagine Marakech, a lamb stew including peaches and prunes.

✉ 48 rue Damiette ☎ 02 35 70 63 58 🕐 Lunch, dinner

La Couronne (££–£££)

Set in a 14th-century Norman building, this famous restaurant in the historic heart of Rouen claims to be the oldest not only in the city but in France. Gourmets are prepared to pay for the excellent food, but it is possible to sample it at slightly lower prices.

✉ 31 place du Vieux-Marché ☎ 02 35 71 40 90 🕐 Lunch, dinner

Dufour (£–££)

Seafood including grilled salmon and mussels; also crêpes and calvados soufflés. Good-value set menus in a restaurant with old-fashioned, unpretentious decor.

✉ 67 bis, rue St Nicolas ☎ 02 35 71 90 62 🕐 Lunch

Écaille (£££)

An up-market restaurant near the place du Vieux-Marché, serving deli-cacies such as lobster salad with ingenious combinations of ingredients. Calvados naturally makes an appearance.

✉ 26 rampe Cauchois ☎ 02 35 70 95 52 🕐 Lunch, dinner. Closed Sat and Sun eve, Mon, 8–25 Aug

Les Garamantes (££)

An informal atmosphere in a cheerfully decorated, small restaurant serving favourite Norman dishes, especially seafood, and other French cuisine. Purple decor, white tablecloths, mirrored walls and lots of locals smoking.

✉ 4 rue Ste-Croix-des-Pelletiers ☎ 02 35 70 56 83 🕐 Lunch, dinner

Gill (££–£££)

Rouennais meals are given a modern touch in this cool,

green, modern building by the Seine. Lobster and pigeon are among the offerings; an experience as well as a good meal.

📧 **9 quai de la Bourse** ☎ **02 35 71 16 14** 🕐 **Lunch, dinner. Closed 13–20 Apr, 3–18 Aug, Sun eve in winter, Mon**

Gourmand'grain (£–££)
A pleasant vegetarian option near the cathedral, serving mainly lunches from a counter tucked into the corner of a health-food shop.

📧 **3 rue Petit Salut** ☎ **02 35 98 15 74** 🕐 **Tue–Sat 10–7. Closed Sun, Mon, 25 Dec–1 Jan, 1–20 Aug**

Kashemir (£)
Tandoori dishes, meat curries, grills and Naan or cheese bread: filling and cheap.

📧 **13 rue Anatole France** ☎ **02 35 71 85 89** 🕐 **Lunch, dinner**

Les Maraîchers (£–££)
Popular old-town restaurant and bistro with tables outside well positioned for watching the world go by. A range of set menus, decent seafood and snails, plus good goat's-cheese salads.

📧 **37 place du Vieux-Marché** ☎ **02 35 71 57 73** 🕐 **Lunch, dinner**

La Mer (£–££)
A seafood restaurant in the old town; one reasonably priced set menu includes coffee and wine.

📧 **14 place du Vieux-Marché** ☎ **02 35 89 88 72** 🕐 **Lunch, dinner**

Nos Viandes Normandes (£)
Restaurant near the Musée des Beaux-Arts, offering several good-value lunchtime menus, with meat dishes such as beef and veal.

📧 **35 rue Jean Lecanuet** ☎ **02 35 71 02 48** 🕐 **Lunch, dinner**

Les Nymphéas (£££)
Upmarket Norman cuisine includes game and fish dishes, plus hot apple and calvados soufflé. Attractive old building with a courtyard, near place du Vieux-Marché.

📧 **7–9 rue de la Pie** ☎ **02 35 89 26 69** 🕐 **Lunch, dinner. Closed 26–30 Aug, Sun eve, Mon**

L'Orangerie (£–££)
An atmospheric, vaulted room and courtyard with plants, statues and a cheerful, comfortable feel. Tables are set outside in spring and summer, and the very reasonable menu includes good seafood.

📧 **2 rue Thomas Corneille** ☎ **02 35 88 43 97** 🕐 **Lunch, dinner**

Le Panda (££)
Tucked away off the road with its own courtyard and an entrance guarded by two Chinese lions. A large, efficient restaurant which packs in the customers and serves generous helpings of Chinese and Vietnamese food.

📧 **4 rue Ste-Croix-des-Pelletiers** ☎ **02 35 89 82 00** 🕐 **Lunch, dinner**

Restaurant des Beaux-Arts (££)
Couscous in a variety of forms, plus grilled food and no-nonsense desserts in an old-fashioned but elegant setting complete with uniformed waiters.

📧 **34 rue Damiette** ☎ **02 35 70 17 15** 🕐 **Lunch, dinner**

Terrasse (££)
A small, attractive restaurant serving meat and some seafood, including the speciality of the house, veal with Camembert. Near the Tour Jeanne d'Arc, in a pink-and-green timber-framed building, with a summer terrace at the back.

📧 **rue Bouvreuil** ☎ **02 35 07 53 23** 🕐 **Dinner**

Time for Tea
Salons de thé are found in most sizeable towns – many decked out with chintzy, rather prim furnishings and decor, and some offering an excellent range of herbal and flavoured teas and snacks. Most open mornings and afternoons and serve 'light lunches' which can actually be fairly substantial. The best have a selection of delicious cakes and pastries. For strong, plain tea ask for 'breakfast'; you may need to ask specifically for milk.

The Northeast

Family Feeding

It's not at all unusual to see family groups, including very young children, sitting down to an evening meal in a restaurant. Children are accepted members of the clientele in French eateries, many of which offer quite extensive reduced-price children's menus.

Caudebec-en-Caux
Normandie (£–£££)
Long established hotel-restaurant next door to the Normotel-la-Marine. Popular for its river views and friendly welcome. The weekday set menu offers good value for money.

✉ 19 quai Guilbaud ☎ 02 35 96 25 11 🕐 Lunch, dinner. Closed Feb

Dieppe
L'Armorique (£–££)
A first-floor restaurant and ground-floor café attached to a fish shop and overlooking the fishing boats. Generous *assiettes de fruits de mer* come in two quantities, enormous and unbelievable, and the menu ranges from simple and cheap to sophisticated and slightly pricier fish dishes.

✉ 17 quai Henri IV ☎ 02 35 84 28 14 🕐 Lunch, dinner. Closed Sun eve, Mon

Marmite Dieppoise (£–££)
Located near Église St-Jacques and the harbour, this popular little seafood restaurant serves the local speciality of bowls heaped with a variety of shellfish.

✉ 8 rue St-Jean ☎ 02 35 84 24 26 🕐 Lunch, dinner. Closed mid-Nov to mid-Dec, late Feb to mid-Mar, Thu in winter, Sun eve, Mon

Étretat
L'Huîtrière (££–£££)
A conspicuous semicircular building under the Falaise d'Aval, housing a restaurant on two floors. Windows take up the entire wall, allowing panoramic sea views. Seafood is the obvious speciality, and comes in enormous quantities.

✉ rue de Traz Perier ☎ 02 35 27 02 82 🕐 Lunch, dinner

Les Roches Blanches (££)
A long, low seafood restaurant on the seafront, with wide picture windows, crouching under the cliff at the Falaise d'Amont end of the bay.

✉ terrasse Boudin, front de la mer ☎ 02 35 27 07 34 🕐 Lunch, dinner

Honfleur
Auberge du Vieux Clocher (££–£££)
A very smart restaurant in a charming alleyway, with an intimate atmosphere and interesting varieties on the seafood theme, as well as lamb, beef and duck dishes.

✉ 9 rue de l'Homme-de-Bois ☎ 02 31 89 12 06 🕐 Lunch, dinner. Closed Jan, Sun eve, Wed

L'Assiette Gourmande (££–£££)
Veal, snails, speciality rice-based dishes and excellent desserts in a prime location near place Ste-Catherine

✉ 2 quai Passagers ☎ 02 31 89 24 88 🕐 Lunch, dinner

Les Bagues d'Argent (£–££)
Colourful decor brightens up an old building with wooden supports and beams. Set in a quiet street away from the harbour. The menu includes prawns and chicken in calvados, spicy beef and *tripes à la mode de Caen*.

✉ 30–32 rue de l'Homme-de-Bois ☎ 02 31 89 27 97 🕐 Lunch, dinner. Closed Tue in winter

La Cidrerie (££)
A *crêperie* that prides itself on traditional *galettes*

and *crepes* prepared 'before your very eyes'. Washed down with cider, *poiré*, *pommeau* or calvados, or one of its own creations such as P'tio Punch or l'Épiscopal.

✉ 26 place Hamelin ☎ 02 31 89 59 85 🕓 Lunch, dinner. Closed Wed

Le Corsaire (£–££)

An intimate dining room in a creamy-yellow old building overlooking the church. Tables are set outside; inside the restaurant is warm and cosy, with an open fire. Squid, chicken in calvados, fish kebabs and guinea fowl braised in calvados among the offerings.

✉ 22 place Ste-Catherine ☎ 02 31 89 12 80 🕓 Lunch, dinner

Hostellerie Lechat (££)

An imposing grey-stone building covered in creepers and overlooking the market place and wooden church. Typical Norman dishes and seafood.

✉ 3 place Ste-Catherine ☎ 02 31 14 49 49 🕓 Closed Wed eve and Thu, and Jan to mid-Feb

La Lieutenance (££)

Outdoor tables in a busy, central position. Good-value lunches and delicious oysters in a no-nonsense style.

✉ 12 place Ste-Catherine ☎ 02 31 89 07 52 🕓 Lunch, dinner. Closed Sun eve in winter, also mid-Nov to mid-Dec

Le Pêle-Mêle (££)

A tea room and *crêperie* that also serves simple meals such as steak and chips, mussels, and omelettes. Small and cosy (only six tables); overlooks busy shops through picture windows. Two entrances.

✉ 96 quai Ste-Catherine/4 rue du Dauphin ☎ 02 31 89 50 45 🕓 Closed evenings

Restaurant le Vieux Honfleur (££–£££)

An old house full of character beside the harbour, with a timber-framed upper storey, tiled floors and wood panelling. Fresh seafood can be enjoyed on the tables outside.

✉ 13 quai St-Étienne ☎ 02 31 89 15 31 🕓 Lunch, dinner. Closed Jan

Lyons-la-Forêt
Le Grand Cerf (££)

A restaurant with rooms in an old market-place inn, which serves fresh ingredients with an original touch, including home-baked cakes and puddings.

✉ place de la Halle ☎ 02 32 49 06 21 🕓 Lunch, dinner. Closed mid-Jan to mid-Feb, Tue, Wed

La Licorne (££–£££)

A restaurant with rooms in a beautiful old pink-and-brown timber-framed building overlooking the historic market hall. Popular and reliable.

✉ place Bensérade ☎ 02 32 49 62 02 🕓 Lunch, dinner. Closed mid-Dec to mid-Jan, Sun eve, Mon in winter

Le Tréport
Le Homard Bleu (££)

One of a huge choice of seafood restaurants along the harbour quay, offering cheaper weekday menus.

✉ 45 quai François 1er ☎ 02 35 86 15 89 🕓 Lunch, dinner. Closed Jan to mid-Feb

Villequier
Grand Sapin (££)

Atmospheric hotel-restaurant with period furniture and balconies overlooking the Seine. Traditional dishes and seafood, using local ingredients. Wood-panelled dining room.

☎ 02 35 56 78 73 🕓 Lunch, dinner. Closed late Nov, mid-Feb to mid-Mar, Tue eve, Wed in winter

Breaking the Habit

The anti-smoking lobby has had some impact even in France, but you are still unlikely to find an entirely smoke-free area in most restaurants and bars. Be prepared to sit within drifting range as diners whet their appetites or round off a meal with a cigarette or cigar.

Caen & Central Normandy

On the Farm

Traditional home-cooked dishes, served in farmhouses that range from the cosily domestic to the grand historic, are offered in Normandy's *fermes-auberges*. As well as using their own farm produce in their (often very stylish) recipes, some proprietors include tours around the farm. A list of *fermes-auberges* is published by Gîtes de France Normandie, 9 rue de la Petite Cité, BP 882 27008 Evreux (☎ 02 32 62 00 80).

Caen

Alcide (£–££)

An affordable and popular option in the town centre. Classic French dishes, bistro-style, are served to a loyal local clientele. Generous helpings of mussels, crêpes and meat dishes.

✉ 1 place Courtonne ☎ 02 31 44 18 06 🕐 Lunch, dinner. Closed late Dec, Sat

L'Amandier (££)

A small, intimate restaurant in a timber-framed building on a narrow street. Candlelit tables and whitewashed stone walls; traditional French dishes.

✉ rue Froide ☎ 02 31 85 33 39 🕐 Lunch, dinner

L'Aubaine (£)

Norman specialities in the old cobbled quarter, including *trou normand*; plain decor, brick and stone walls, wrought-iron embellishments.

✉ rue Porte Auberge ☎ 02 31 93 26 00 🕐 Lunch, dinner

La Bourride (££–£££)

The most highly regarded restaurant in Caen, with prices to match. Set in one of the older sections of Caen, its decor of copper utensils and flowers complements stone walls and a cosy fire. Regional specialities include Caen *tripes*, chicken in creamy *vallée d'Auge* sauce, Vire chitterlings, pigs' trotters *galette* and other stylish dishes – each guaranteed to have their own added unique touches.

✉ 15–17 rue du Vaugueux ☎ 02 31 93 50 76 🕐 Lunch, dinner. Closed mid-Aug to 3 Sep, Jan, Sun eve, Mon

Le Dauphin (£–£££)

Great food using local ingredients served in a former priory, now a restaurant-with-rooms near the château and abbeys. The smart dining room has a welcoming atmosphere and a wide range of price options. Narrow stairways, exposed beams and stonework.

✉ 29 rue Gémare ☎ 02 31 86 22 26 🕐 Lunch, dinner. Closed 28 Jan–12 Feb, mid-Jul to early Aug, Sat lunch

La Maison Italie (£)

A small, friendly and informal pizzeria serving the standard fare of Italian and international dishes. Open every night of the week.

✉ 10 rue Hamon ☎ 02 31 86 38 02 🕐 Lunch, dinner

Le Palais Impérial (£–££)

Chinese food in a comfortable restaurant on a busy road near the château. Good food but the service is slow.

✉ avenue de la Libération ☎ 02 31 95 64 96 🕐 Lunch, dinner

Le Paquebot (£)

Smart French cooking in the courtyard of Ancien Abbaye des Croisiers. Very good-value establishment.

✉ 7 rue des Croisiers ☎ 02 31 85 10 10 🕐 Lunch, dinner. Closed Sun

Le Pressoir (£–££)

A pleasant place with 'olde-worlde' touches and straightforward dishes, including local favourites such as *boudin noir* and seafood.

✉ 3 avenue Henri-Chéron ☎ 02 31 73 32 71 🕐 Lunch, dinner. Closed Aug, Sun eve, Mon

Le Quatre Épices (£)

West African dishes include chicken with lemon and onions and a wide range of other meat options, served in a cheerfully decorated old-quarter restaurant.

✉ rue Porte Auberge ☎ 02 31 93 40 41 🕐 Lunch, dinner

Restaurant Kouba (£–££)

Atmospheric restaurant in the old quarter, with camel murals and North African muzak to accompany the generous couscous and *tadjine* options.

✉ 6 rue du Vaugueux ☎ 02 31 93 68 47 🕐 Lunch, dinner

Central Normandy

Alençon

La Couscouserie (££)

North African cuisine in a small restaurant opposite Église St-Léonard.

✉ 22 rue St-Léonard ☎ 02 33 32 20 26 🕐 Lunch, dinner

Au Jardin Gourmand (£)

Traditional menu with home-made bread. Located between the historic château and the Sarthe river.

✉ 49 rue de Granges ☎ 02 33 32 22 56 🕐 Lunch, dinner. Closed Sat lunch, Sun eve, Mon

Au Petit Vatel (££)

Locals flock to this friendly restaurant on the edge of town for its charm and good, hearty, traditional food, which includes excellent puddings and an interesting selection of fish dishes.

✉ 72 place Cdt Desmeulles ☎ 02 33 26 23 78 🕐 Lunch, dinner. Closed first three weeks Aug, Feb hols, Sun eve, Wed

Arromanches-les-Bains

La Marine (£–££)

A small hotel-restaurant overlooking the port, with good seafood. Customers receive friendly attention, and can expect high standards of cuisine.

✉ 2 quai Canada ☎ 02 31 22 34 19 🕐 Lunch, dinner. Closed mid-Nov to mid-Feb

Balleroy

Manoir de la Drôme (£££)

Set on the outskirts of the village, this a top-class restaurant that offers a less pricey set menu. Excellent game and fish dishes and imaginative desserts (try the *tarte au chocolat*) use Norman ingredients but with a stylish flourish.

✉ 129 rue Forges ☎ 02 31 21 60 94 🕐 Lunch, dinner. Closed early Sep, Feb, Sun eve, Mon

Bayeux

Le Lion d'Or (££–£££)

An ancient coaching inn near Église St-Jean and assembly rooms. The traditional menu is accompanied by a very good range of wines. A long-established and popular choice with tourists.

✉ 71 rue St-Jean ☎ 02 31 92 06 90 🕐 Lunch, dinner. Closed mid-Dec to mid-Jan

Beuvron-en-Auge

Pavé d'Auge (££–£££)

Set in a timber-framed market building in the village centre, serving pan-fried oysters, speciality lamb dishes, meat with cider, and calvados soufflé desserts.

✉ place du Village ☎ 02 31 79 26 71 🕐 Lunch, dinner. Closed Dec, early Feb, Tue (Sep–Apr), Mon

Brionne

Auberge du Vieux Donjon (££)

Excellent restaurant-with-rooms in an 18th-century inn on the main street of the village. Prettily decorated with flowers and warmed by a real fire. The menu includes superb seafood.

✉ 19 rue de la Soie ☎ 02 32 44 80 62 🕐 Lunch, dinner. Closed late Oct, late Jan, Sun eve in winter

Welcome Inn

Another variation on the country cooking theme is the *auberge du terroir*, or country inn. The best of these offer hearty regional cooking, often in buildings which are worth visiting for their own character and setting. Look out for signs (sometimes in the most remote rural areas) directing you to the local inn, or take your pick from the recommended *auberges* within each *département* – details from Gîtes de France Normandie (➤ 96, panel) or from the Comité Régional du Tourisme de Normandie, 14 rue Charles Corbeau, 27000 Évreux (☎ 02 32 33 79 00).

Brasseries
Less formal and more flexible than traditional restaurants, most brasseries stay open until late at night; some keep going until early morning. Meals are usually quick and filling – though many are not necessarily at prices lower than you would expect to pay at a restaurant.

Deauville
Le Spinnaker (££–£££)
One of the less exclusive eateries in this moneyed resort, which does at least offer a set menu at moderate prices, as well as expensive à-la-carte options.
✉ 52 rue Mirabeau ☎ 02 31 88 24 40 🕒 Lunch, dinner. Closed 12–21 Nov, Jan, Tue, Wed

Dives-sur-Mer
Dupont (££)
A pretty *pâtisserie* – right next to the church – with a tiny *salon de thé* at the back. Simple meals (pâté, pizza, etc), or take your pick from the delicious offerings in the shop.
✉ rue Hélène Boucher ☎ 02 31 91 04 30 🕒 Lunch, afternoon tea

Évreux
Café des Arts (£)
Traditional bar meals, including the obligatory *croque-monsieur/madame* (hefty sandwiches) and a selection of grills and chef's salads. Set in an attractive corner building with views of the belfry and central square.
✉ 5 rue de l'Horloge ☎ 02 32 31 12 52 🕒 Lunch

Camomille (££)
A *salon de thé* serving omelettes and generous salads at lunchtimes, plus ice creams and a wide range of speciality teas, in a prettily decorated though slightly cramped room.
✉ 23 rue de Grenoble ☎ 02 32 38 30 90 🕒 Lunch. Closed Sun

Le Jardin d'Élodie (£–££)
Picture windows give great views of the cathedral. Clean and spacious decor and a menu including duck, veal, seafood and snails.
✉ 11 rue de la Harpe ☎ 02 32 38 08 66 🕒 Lunch, dinner. Closed Mon in winter

Restaurant Michel Thomas (£–££)
Norman specialities with an individual touch – duck, veal, and inventive desserts such as spicy fruit puddings. Served in a smart, quiet building on a busy shopping street.
✉ 87 rue Joséphine ☎ 02 32 33 05 70 🕒 Lunch, dinner. Closed Sun

Orbec
L'Orbecquoise (££–£££)
A quiet, cosy restaurant with a log fire, serving stylishly prepared Norman specialities, with a range of reasonable set menus.
✉ 60 rue Grande ☎ 02 31 62 44 99 🕒 Lunch, dinner

Trouville
La Guinguette (£–££)
Seafood, fish dishes and *tripes à la mode de Caen* served in a friendly small restaurant with pavement tables, overlooking the river and fishing boats.
✉ 50–52 quai Fernand Moureaux ☎ 02 31 88 42 80 🕒 Lunch, dinner

La Marine (£–££)
Mussels, crabs, prawns and other seafood in a restaurant opposite the fish market. Stone and brick walls; dark, traditional decor.
✉ 146 boulevard Fernand Moureaux ☎ 02 31 88 12 51 🕒 Lunch, dinner

Les Mouettes (£–££)
Pleasant corner restaurant, set in a quiet location away from the river and beach. Good seafood.
✉ 9–11 rue des Bains ☎ 02 31 98 06 97 🕒 Lunch, dinner

La Moulerie (£–££)
All manner of *moules*, including *moules Normande*, in a riverside restaurant.
✉ 76 boulevard Fernand Moureaux ☎ 02 31 81 59 00 🕒 Lunch, dinner

The Northwest

Barfleur

Hôtel Moderne (££)

Restaurant-with-rooms serving speciality salmon dishes, oysters and goat's-cheese *millefeuille*. Cheaper set menu during the week.

✉ 1 place De Gaulle ☎ 02 33 23 12 44 🕙 Lunch, dinner. Closed mid-Jan to mid-Mar, Wed mid-Sep to mid-Jan, Tue Sep–Jun

Barneville-Carteret

Hôtel de la Marine (£££)

Pricey but stylish restaurant in a hotel; oysters with innovative sauces, local lamb, and vanilla butter with cinnamon and sweet cider.

✉ 11 rue de Paris ☎ 02 33 53 83 31 🕙 Lunch, dinner. Closed Sun eve and Mon Feb, Mar and Oct, Mon lunch Jul–Aug

Cherbourg

Café de Paris (£–££)

Live lobsters in tanks; very good range of seafood dishes and a good value set menu, in a café overlooking the port.

✉ 40 quai de Caligny ☎ 02 33 43 12 36 🕙 Lunch, dinner. Closed early Nov

Le Grandgousier (££–£££)

Charming rosy decor and stylish but friendly service. Classy touches are given to a wide range of seafood options, including caviar, crab claws, shellfish and salmon.

✉ 21 rue de l'Abbaye ☎ 02 33 53 19 43 🕙 Lunch, dinner

Hôtel La Régence (££)

Restaurant in the hotel of the same name on the quay. Straightforward fish and meat dishes served in brasserie-style room with large windows.

✉ 42 quai de Caligny ☎ 02 33 43 05 16 🕙 Lunch, dinner

Granville

La Gentilhommière (££–£££)

An established restaurant near the harbourside, serving traditional French dishes. Space is limited: book ahead.

✉ 152 rue Couraye ☎ 02 33 50 17 99 🕙 Lunch, dinner. Closed early Mar, Sun eve, Mon in winter

Phare (£–££)

Mussels and various fish combinations, including Chausey lobsters and a vast seafood basket. Service can be sluggish but patience will be rewarded.

✉ 11 rue du Port ☎ 02 33 50 12 94 🕙 Lunch, dinner. Closed Tue eve, Wed

Le Mont-St-Michel

Hôtel la Croix Blanche (£–££)

A well-placed hotel-restaurant (➤ 105) with good food at reasonable prices, and omelettes to compete with the famous Poulard version (➤ below).

✉ Grande Rue ☎ 02 33 60 14 04 🕙 Lunch, dinner. Closed mid-Nov to Dec

La Mère Poulard (££–£££)

Famous hotel-restaurant, with renowned omelettes made to the recipe devised by Mme Poulard in the late 19th century. Bay views.

✉ Grande Rue ☎ 02 33 60 14 01 🕙 Lunch, dinner

St-Lô

Hôtel les Voyageurs (£–££)

The hotel's restaurant serves stylish meals.

✉ 5 avenue Briovère ☎ 02 33 05 08 63 🕙 Lunch, dinner

Get Set

Restaurants tend to display a range of set menus (*menus fixes*) outside; don't be afraid to study the options before committing yourself. Even the most up-market places may offer quite reasonably priced menus, with a fixed number of courses and a limited choice (the cheaper the menu, the less choice you have). Some include wine and coffee. Weekday lunchtime menus can often give exceptionally good value.

99

Rouen

Prices
Ratings are based on prices per room, per night.
£ = under €30.5 (F200)
££ = €30.50–61 (F200–400)
£££ = over €61 (F400)

Gîtes de France
If you prefer to get off the hotel-motel circuit, it's worth looking at the different types of accommodation offered by Gîtes de France. These include houses or cottages (*gîtes*), often with real character and charm, in isolated rural areas or on the coast, which you can rent for self-catering weeks or a weekend. Details are available from Gîtes de France, Maison du Département, 50008 St-Lô (02 33 05 98 70).

Le Bristol (££)
Overlooking the Palais de Justice and near the rue du Gros-Horloge. Comfortable rooms and parking – a great asset in this largely pedestrianised part of town.
45 rue aux Juifs 02 35 71 54 21

Le Dandy (££)
Well positioned on the rue Cauchoise, leading off to the north of the place du Vieux-Marché, this small hotel is handy for the old-town sights. No restaurant, but near the most popular eateries.
93 rue Cauchoise 02 35 07 32 00

Frantour Rouen Vieux-Marché (£££)
A popular and convenient hotel very near the place du Vieux-Marché but assertively modern, with glass walls overlooking a courtyard and simple, stylish comfort inside. No restaurant.
33 rue du Vieux Palais 02 35 71 00 88

Hôtel des Arcades (£–££)
A good basic hotel in a busy street lined with shops and fast-food restaurants. Some rooms have bath or shower, others just a toilet and bidet.
52 rue des Carmes 02 35 70 10 30

Hôtel de la Cathédrale (££)
An old building with a pretty courtyard and green-and-white decor, near the cathedral and archbishop's palace. Not easily accessible by car, but a place of genuine character – among some of Rouen's best medieval houses – and run with friendly, attentive charm. No restaurant.
12 rue St-Romain 02 35 71 57 95

Hôtel de Dieppe (£££)
All mod cons in this Best Western hotel with a highly reputable restaurant, Le Quatre Saisons.
place B Tissot 02 35 71 96 00

Hôtel Mercure Rouen Centre (£££)
A discreetly up-market hotel in the Mercure chain, with a large, open lobby behind sliding doors in a narrow old-town street. Facilities include a private garage and all mod cons in the rooms. No restaurant.
7 rue Croix-de-Fer 02 35 52 69 52

Hôtel de Québec (£–££)
Good value in this comfortable hotel run with efficiency; particularly popular with British visitors. Car park.
18–24 rue du Québec 02 35 70 09 38 Closed 23 Dec–3 Jan

Hôtel le Viking (££)
A good bet for an overnight stay. Set on a busy riverside road, but rooms at the rear, overlooking the bus station, are much quieter. Small rooms with all the basics; clean and convenient; helpful service. Locked underground garage.
21 quai du Havre 02 35 70 34 95

Le Vieux Logis (£)
A good budget option, with plain comfort and a restaurant, car park and garden.
5 rue Joyeuse 02 35 71 55 30

The Northeast

Les Andelys
Hôtel de Paris (££)
A handsome, red-brick 19th-century building on the approach road into Grand Andely, with a restaurant.
✉ 10 avenue de la République ☎ 02 32 54 00 33 🕐 Closed Feb

Caudebec-en-Caux
Hôtel St-Philippe (£–££)
Small hotel with views of the Seine. No restaurant.
✉ 4 place d'Armes ☎ 02 35 96 23 01

No 1 Cavée St-Léger (££)
A lovely cottage offering three rooms for bed-and-breakfast, each with its own shower and toilet. Beautifully maintained garden.
✉ 68 rue République ☎ 02 35 96 10 15

Hôtel de Normandie (£–££)
An established hotel-restaurant (Logis de France) with rooms overlooking the river; reasonably priced.
✉ 19 quai Guilbaud ☎ 02 35 96 25 11 🕐 Closed 5–25 Feb

Normotel-La Marine (££)
Balconied hotel-restaurant with good views of the Seine. Parking.
✉ 18 quai Guilbaud ☎ 02 35 96 20 11

Clères
Le Tôt (££)
Bed and breakfast in one double room, in Véronique Degonse's turn-of-the-century home surrounded by 3ha of wooded grounds. Cycle hire.
✉ 76690 Clères ☎ 02 35 33 34 38

Duclair
Hôtel de la Poste (££–£££)
A Logis de France on the Seine quayside. Good first-floor restaurant and a friendly atmosphere.
✉ 286 quai de la Libération ☎ 02 35 05 92 50

Étretat
Hôtel Dormy House (££–£££)
Sea views from this Logis de France with a restaurant.
✉ route du Havre ☎ 02 35 27 07 88

L'Escale (££)
A no-frills hotel with attractive rooms and a small restaurant serving simple meals. Sea views.
✉ place Foch ☎ 02 35 27 03 69

Hôtel les Falaises (£–££)
No sea view, but comfortable, clean rooms in a central position, by the halles. The pink neon sign is unmissable.
✉ 1 boulevard René Coty ☎ 02 35 27 02 77

Hôtel de Normandie (££)
Very comfortable rooms and a pleasant restaurant with open log fire. Large bathrooms, well-equipped with facilities for residents with disabilities.
✉ place Foch ☎ 02 35 27 06 99

Hôtel de la Poste (££)
Simple but efficient hotel offering good value on the town's main road. There is a garden.
✉ 6 avenue George V ☎ 02 35 27 01 34

Hôtel la Résidence (££–£££)
A dark, timber-framed house with a range of comforts. La Tricorne brasserie.
✉ 4 boulevard René Coty ☎ 02 35 27 02 87

Bed and Breakfast
Bed and breakfast is offered in a growing number of private homes, farms, manor houses and even châteaux. Known as *chambres d'hôtes*, they are graded by Gîtes de France in *épis*, or ears of corn: one for simple rooms with basin and shared bathroom; two for comfier rooms with bath or shower and shared toilet; three for fully en-suite rooms; and four for especially comfortable, well-equipped rooms of particular character. Brochures are available from Gîtes de France (► 100, panel).

For the Children
Another variation on the *gîtes* theme is the Gîtes d'Enfants. Members of this scheme welcome children aged between six and twelve into their own families, offering them the opportunity of sampling life in the French countryside. Details from Gîtes de France (➤ 100).

Eu
Domaine de Joinville (£££)
One for special occasions, a *château-hôtel* with tennis, pool, gardens and a gym. Rooms are expensive but the restaurant has reasonably priced options. Meals can be eaten outside on the terrace.
✉ route du Tréport, 1km west ☎ 02 35 50 52 52

Ferme du Viaduc (££)
René Devillepoix offers bed and breakfast at his quiet farmhouse, 3km from le Tréport. One double room, one for three people, each with bathroom and toilet.
✉ 54 rue des Canadiens ☎ 02 35 86 09 69

Hôtel de la Gare (££)
Comfortable rooms in a faded Logis de France near the railway station. Parking.
✉ 20 place de la Gare ☎ 02 35 86 16 64 🕑 Closed 15 Aug–8 Sep

Gisors
Hostellerie des Trois Poissons (£–££)
Impressive timber-framed building on the lively main street, between the church and the château.
✉ 13 rue Cappeville ☎ 02 32 55 01 09 🕑 Summer (except last half of Jun) until Oct.

Le Havre
Clarine Hôtel-Restaurant (££)
A sprawling glass building near the main road and harbour, with a McDonald's next door. Rooms offer good facilities and convenience for travellers.
✉ quai Colbert ☎ 02 35 26 49 49

Honfleur
L'Absinthe (£££)
An up-market and expensive hotel set in a former 16th-century presbytery in the old town. Comfortable, characterful rooms with exposed beams. The restaurant has reasonably priced set menus.
✉ 10 quai de la Quarantaine ☎ 02 31 89 23 23 🕑 Closed 14 Nov–31 Dec

Hôtel Campanile (££)
Modern motel-style accommodation with restaurant, on the D579 just outside town. Buffet breakfasts, en-suite bedrooms with coffee- and tea-making facilities, rooms for visitors with disabilities, and non-smoking rooms. Plenty of free parking.
✉ le Poundreux Route de Paris ☎ 02 31 89 13 13

Hôtel des Cascades (££)
Reasonable prices in a central position set back from the Vieux Bassin on a cobbled street. Cheerful, good-value restaurant.
✉ 17 place Thiers (cours de Fossés) ☎ 02 31 89 05 83 🕑 Closed 12 Nov–14 Feb

Hôtel du Dauphin (££–£££)
An old timber-framed building in the centre of the bustling town. Rather old-fashioned lounge bar downstairs overlooking the street. Wide range of prices.
✉ 10 place Berthelot ☎ 02 31 89 15 53 🕑 Closed Jan

Otelinn (££)
A modern hotel with comfortable, small rooms and a traditional-style restaurant serving local dishes. About a kilometre from the Vieux Bassin. Free parking.
✉ 62 cours Albert-Manuel ☎ 02 31 89 41 77

Le Tréport
Le Saint-Yves (£–££)
A friendly, traditional resort hotel with flowery decor and a restaurant serving good-value seafood.
✉ 7 place Albert Cauët ☎ 02 35 86 34 66 🕑 Closed mid-Dec to mid-Jan

Caen & Central Normandy

Caen

Au Saint-Jean (£–££)
Good-value rooms with no frills but all basic facilities; helpful staff and its own garage. Near the Église St-Jean, south of the château.
✉ 20 rue des Martyrs ☎ 02 31 86 23 35

Central Hôtel (£)
A hotel that lives up to its name, being well placed in the city centre, with views of the château from some rooms. Cheap and basic, but convenient. No restaurant.
✉ 23 place J Letellier ☎ 02 31 86 18 52

Hôtel Alcide (££)
Cheerful decor – smart and simple – in a popular hotel (with bistro-style restaurant) near the quay.
✉ 1 place Courtonne ☎ 02 31 44 18 06

Hôtel des Cordeliers (£–££)
Wide range of rooms with a choice of prices. Set in its own garden.
✉ 4 rue des Cordeliers ☎ 02 31 86 37 15

Hôtel Courtonne (£)
A cheaper option than the upmarket Mercure in the same square (► below). Plain, clean rooms, parking. Near the Tour le Roy.
✉ 5 rue des Prairies St-Gilles ☎ 02 31 93 47 83

Hôtel le Dauphin (££–£££)
A restored 18th-century priory with rooms in the old building and a modern annexe. Traditional, country-style restaurant. Car park.
✉ 29 rue Gémare ☎ 02 31 86 22 26

Mercure Caen Centre (£££)
High prices for reliable en-suite rooms with all the trappings, including colour TV with international channels, minibars. Buffet breakfasts, atrium bar. On a square at the northern end of the Pleasure Port.
✉ 1 place Courtonne ☎ 02 31 47 24 24

Hôtel Moderne (££–£££)
Set in the long boulevard leading into the place St-Pierre (for the tourist office and church), this pleasant hotel also has its own car park. Not particularly modern in appearance, though, and difficult to reach by car: ask for directions. No restaurant.
✉ 116 boulevard Maréchal Leclerc ☎ 02 31 86 04 23

Hôtel des Quatrans (£–££)
Well-signposted hotel in an alley near the centre. Pastel decor, clean and comfortable rooms (some without showers). No restaurant.
✉ 17 rue Gémare ☎ 02 31 86 25 57

Hôtel Saint-Étienne (£)
A good budget choice with character, set in an 18th-century stone building within reach of the Abbaye aux Hommes. Some rooms without showers.
✉ 2 rue de l'Académie ☎ 02 31 86 35 82

Hôtel de l'Univers (£–££)
Small and basic motel near the quayside, with rather drearily decorated but clean rooms, some sharing toilet facilities. Set on a large and busy square with plenty of public parking.
✉ 12 quai Vendeuvre, place Courtonne ☎ 02 31 85 46 14

Laying on the Charm
If money is no object, consider spending on a stay in Normandy's up-market 'hotels of charm' set in grand châteaux, rambling country inns, converted mills or turreted manor-houses. Many have gourmet restaurants, too. A booklet called *Hôtels-Restaurants de Charme en Normandie* is published by the Comité Régional de Tourisme de Normandie at Le Doyenné, 14 rue Charles Corbeau, Évreux (☎ 02 32 33 79 00).

Logis de France

Hotels that tag Logis de France or LF after their names are part of a voluntary association – now with over 3,800 members – that guarantees a high level of comfort and service, excellent food, and a pleasant environment. Each hotel's range of facilities is graded with one, two or three *cheminées* (fireplaces). Details are available from the Fédération Nationale des Logis de France, 83 avenue d'Italie, 75013 Paris (01 45 84 70 00).

Central Normandy

Alençon

Hôtel Le Chapeau Rouge (£–££)

Convenient and pretty hotel in the heart of town. Some rooms overlooking the adjacent road can be noisy. No restaurant.

 1 and 3 boulevard Duchamp
 02 33 26 20 23 Closed 1–15 Aug

Hôtel Le Grand St-Michel (£–££)

Good-value, traditional service in a quiet Logis de France hotel. Restaurant serves generous portions for very reasonable prices.

 7 rue du Temple 02 33 26 04 77 Closed 3–30 Jul, 29 Oct–23 Nov, 1 Jan–5 Mar

Bayeux

Hôtel du Lion d'Or (££–£££)

Long-established hotel in an old coaching inn with a courtyard, near the centre. Bright, comfortable rooms and a restaurant.

 71 rue St-Jean 02 31 92 06 90 Closed 17 Nov–18 Jan

Hôtel Mogador (££)

A very pleasant hotel tucked in among the shops, with a friendly welcome and good-value rooms, some of which have cooking facilities.

 20 rue Alain Chartier
 02 31 92 24 58

Hôtel Notre-Dame (£–££)

Welcoming hotel with very reasonable prices, well placed within view of the cathedral. Restaurant.

 44 rue des Cuisiniers
 02 31 92 87 24

Cabourg

Grand Hôtel (£££)

An up–market seafront hotel in the grand old tradition, which makes the most of its connections with Proust, and serves *madeleines* (the cakes associated with his *Remembrance of Things Past*) for breakfast.

 promenade Marcel Proust
 02 31 91 01 79

Hôtel de Paris (£–££)

Central hotel in a timber-framed building, with a wide range of room prices. Parking.

 39 avenue de la Mer
 02 31 91 31 34

Évreux

France (££)

A traditional hotel set in a quiet location within the centre of Évreux. The pleasant rooms are augmented by a very good restaurant offering classic dishes and fine wines.

 29 rue St-Thomas 02 32 39 09 25

Sées

Hôtel du Cheval Blanc (£–££)

Some of the rooms at the back of this timber-framed building are rather dark and oppressive. Others are brighter with good views of the cathedral.

 1 place St-Pierre 02 33 27 80 48 Closed 16–27 Feb, 11 Nov–31 Dec

Hôtel Le Dauphin (££)

Logis de France hotel near the old market hall, with good breakfasts and generous evening meals.

 31 place des Halles 02 33 27 80 07 Closed Jan

Trouville

Hôtel Carmen (££–£££)

A small hotel near the beach, with a friendly atmosphere.

 24 rue Carnot 02 31 88 35 43 Closed Jan

Hôtel les Sablettes (££)

Quiet hotel with a garden, near the town centre.

 15 rue P Besson 02 31 88 10 66

The Northwest

Barneville-Carteret

Hôtel de la Marine (£££)
Cheerful hotel overlooking the sea and port. Expensive rooms; terrace with parasol tables in summer. Parking and an excellent restaurant.
✉ **11 rue de Paris** ☎ **02 33 53 83 31** 🕐 **Closed 3 Nov–19 Feb**

Cherbourg

Ambassadeur Hôtel (£–££)
Bright, well-designed rooms, double-glazed against the busy port near by. Parking behind the hotel. Restaurant.
✉ **22 quai de Caligny** ☎ **02 33 43 10 00**

Hôtel Mercure (£££)
Modern building, strangely isolated beside the port. Convenient for the car ferry, but less so for the town centre and restaurants.
✉ **Allée Président Menut** ☎ **02 33 44 01 11**

Hôtel la Régence (££–£££)
Pleasant Logis de France hotel in a white quayside building, with simply furnished rooms, parking at the rear, and a brasserie-style restaurant.
✉ **42 quai de Caligny** ☎ **02 33 43 05 16** 🕐 **Closed 24 Dec–2 Jan**

Coutances

Hôtel le Normandie (£–££)
Small hotel behind the cathedral, with a restaurant (closed Mon in winter, Sun eve) serving good-value meals. Parking.
✉ **2 place Général-de-Gaulle** ☎ **02 33 45 01 40**

Granville

Hôtel le Grand Large (££–£££)
Modern building set on the cliff overlooking the sea; includes a sea-therapy centre. Parking, swimming pool, jacuzzi, restaurant. Wide price range for rooms.
✉ **5 rue de la Falaise** ☎ **02 33 91 19 19**

Le Mont-St-Michel

Hôtel la Croix Blanche (££–£££)
Well-known hotel on the ramparts with spectacular views of the bay and a restaurant offering some good-value menus (► 99). Rooms, however, can be expensive.
✉ **Intra-Muros** ☎ **02 33 60 14 04** 🕐 **Closed 16 Nov–14 Feb**

Hôtel du Mouton Blanc (££–£££)
Attractive stone and timber building, with a good restaurant and sea views. The cheapest rooms – by the standards of le Mont-St-Michel – are very reasonable.
✉ **Intra-Muros** ☎ **02 33 60 14 08**

Orbec

Chambres Mme Vaillère (£–££)
Excellent bed and breakfast in an old house on the main street. Double rooms in an annexe (two share bathroom and toilet) entered through a pretty courtyard. Breakfast served inside or out. Evening meals by arrangement.
✉ **62 rue Grande** ☎ **02 31 32 77 99**

Villedieu-les-Poëles

Hôtel le Fruitier (££)
Well-run Logis de France hotel and restaurant, open all year. Modern, com-fortable rooms with stylish decor and welcoming staff.
✉ **place des Costils** ☎ **02 33 90 51 00**

Access to Accommodation

Few tourist sites in Normandy are fully prepared for visitors with disabilities, but there are some associations offering guidance about finding suitable accommodation. *Les Gîtes accessibles aux personnes handicapées* is published by Gîtes de France and is available from 35 rue Godot de Mauroy, 75439 Paris; and the *Guide Rousseau*, which covers hotels, bed and breakfast, *gîtes*, and camping sites by *département*, is available from Association France H, 9 rue Luce de Lancival, 77340 Pontault-Combault.

Gifts

Shopping Glossary

la boulangerie bakery, selling the traditional 'stick' bread (*baguette*) plus a wide variety of types of loaf (*pain*)
le boucherie butcher
les cadeaux gifts
la charcuterie ham, sausages, pork and snacks (meat or fish pies)
la chocolaterie/confiserie chocolates and sweetmeats
l'épicerie grocery
la fromagerie cheese shop
la librairie bookshop, newsagent
la pâtisserie pastries, almost always fresh and delicious, ranging from the relatively plain, such as croissants, to the elaborate and creamy
la pharmacie chemist
la poissonerie fishmonger
le tabac tobacconist (also sells stamps)

Rouen

Arte Verre
Original ceramics in bold modern designs; also glassware and lights.
✉ rue Ganterie ☎ 02 35 70 14 06

Bleu Cactus
Interesting jewellery and other gifts such as clocks and keyrings, in intriguing modern designs.
✉ rue Ganterie ☎ 02 35 71 55 55

Chasset Patrick
Antiques including toy cars, dolls, furniture and crockery. Opposite the upmarket Hôtel Mercure.
✉ rue de la Croix de Fer ☎ 02 35 70 59 97

Cosy Casa
Attractive gifts for the home, including painted screens, lamps, glassware and objets d'art.
✉ 55 rue St-Nicolas ☎ 02 35 70 60 20

Faïence d'Art
Opposite Église St-Maclou, an upmarket shop specialising in clocks – ceramic, wooden, big and small – and faience gifts.
✉ place Barthélemy ☎ 02 35 71 58 34

La Fontaine Marmitaine
A very attractive toyshop in a timber-framed building, with displays of rocking horses, puppets, dolls, toy soldiers and teddy bears in its large picture window.
✉ rue du Gros-Horloge ☎ 02 35 88 19 99

Ma Normandie
In the heart of the old town, specialising in faience (decorated ceramics) in the form of ornaments, pots and plates. Other gifts include pictures and barometers.
✉ Corner of rue St-Nicolas ☎ 02 35 71 46 08

The Northeast

Dieppe
Antiquités Sutton
Antique cutlery, porcelain figures and ivory pieces in a corner shop.
✉ rue St-Rémy

Le Comptoir des Isles/Le Gallion
Jewellery and gifts with a maritime theme – toy boats, floating-ship paperweights, and ship wheels and lamps.
✉ place Nationale ☎ 02 35 40 14 18

La Galerie Montador
Art gallery and children's gift and toy shop, with wooden trains, puppets and bricks, Tintin tee shirts, and grown-ups' gifts such as lamps and ship-shape condiments.
✉ 4 rue Bains ☎ 02 35 82 63 03

Honfleur
Bijoux Minéraux
Dazzling display of precious stones, used in jewels and ornaments, plus polished fossils.
✉ rue St-Antoine

Domin R et Fils
Crammed with gifts, ornaments, penknives, thimbles, ships in bottles and every other conceivable knick-knack. Overlooks the harbour.
✉ rue de la République ☎ 02 31 89 05 52

Le Sémaphore

Ship compasses and bells, lanterns, sailor's caps, porthole mirrors, and other gifts for the seadog who has everything.

✉ rue des Lingots ☎ 02 31 89 97 85

Caen

Artagor

Arts and crafts, including mosaic mirrors, painted lamps, hats and jewellery – unusual souvenirs.

✉ rue Buquet ☎ 02 31 93 16 00

Le Bois Dormant

Wonderful wooden toys and games for children – tops, trains, drums, jigsaws – in the traditional style. The shop is opposite Église St-Sauveur.

✉ rue Froide ☎ 02 31 85 35 01

Leblon-Delienne

Inventive gifts based on characters such as Tintin, and Wallace and Gromit, including pictures, models, ties and underwear; plus stylish lamps and ornaments.

✉ rue Froide ☎ 02 31 85 70 70

Central Normandy

Alençon
Fred

The name is from the orthopaedic clinic upstairs. A lovely selection of modern gifts, from lamps to statuettes, furniture to flowers, on the corner of passage de la Briante.

✉ rue aux Sieurs ☎ 02 33 81 14 20

Bayeux
La Boutique

Carved wooden boxes, ceramics, jewellery, candles and other gifts.

✉ 29 rue St-Jean

Évreux
L'Île ô Perle

Jewellery, watches, craft kits, and unusual stone and ceramic ornaments in a shop-cum-workshop, where the owner keeps busy producing new items. Located in the shopping centre off rue Chartraine.

✉ Galeries Chartraine ☎ 02 32 33 42 52

Tentations

Painted wooden ornaments, jewellery, umbrellas and other gift ideas.

✉ rue Docteur Oursel ☎ 02 32 31 66 65

Trouville
Art et Decoration

Painted pots, lights, pictures and gifts, some tacky, others interesting, in a little riverside shop.

✉ boulevard Fernand-Moureaux

Miel Marine

Rugs, crockery, interesting household gifts, candelabra – all in simple but effective designs.

✉ rue des Bains ☎ 02 31 81 17 96

The Northwest

Cherbourg
A Cosnefroy

Textiles, umbrellas, lamps, dolls; all kinds of everything in a cluttered but welcoming little shop.

✉ 18 rue au Blé ☎ 02 33 93 19 27

Villedieu-les-Poëles
A la Main d'Or

One of a clutch of shops on the high street selling pots, pans, kettles, lamps, kitchenware and a range of other items made of copper and tin in the Villedieu workshops. Pot seekers are spoilt for choice.

✉ 14 rue Général-de-Gaulle ☎ 02 33 90 62 74

Markets

Weekly markets take place in many Normandy towns and add considerably to their character and atmosphere. Among the regular morning markets are those at Alençon (Tue, Thu, Sat, Sun), Les Andelys (Sat), Argentan (Tue, Fri, Sun), Avranches (Sat), Bayeux (Sat), Bernay (Sat), Brionne (Sun), Caen (Fri, Sun), Cherbourg (Tue), Coutances (Thu), Dieppe (Sat), Dives-sur-Mer (Tue), Étretat (Thu), Eu (Fri) Évreux (Wed, Sat), Fécamp (Sat), Gisors (Mon), Granville (Sat), Honfleur (Sat), Louviers (Sat), Lyons-la-Forêt (Thu), Mortain (Sat), Pont-Audemer (Mon), St-Lô (Sat), Ste-Mère-Eglise (Thu), Sées (Sat), Trouville (Wed, Sun), Valognes (Fri), Verneuil-sur-Avre (Sat), Villedieu-les-Poëles (Tue) and Vire (Fri).

Fashion

What's in Store
Printemps and Monoprix are department-store chains with outlets all over France. Printemps sells mid-budget clothes, jewellery, shoes and cosmetics; Monoprix sells lower-budget clothes, household goods, cosmetics and food. Stores can be found in Rouen, Évreux, Vernon, Lisieux, Trouville, Caen, Cherbourg and other centres.

Rouen

Carlton Cordonnerie
Basically a cobbler's shop, but it also sells *sabots* – big wooden clogs – in a variety of designs for men and women, including very original modern versions.
✉ **rue St-Nicolas** ☎ **02 35 70 22 87**

Catimini
Pretty children's clothes in eye-catching colours and designs; also shoes and accessories.
✉ **50 rue des Carmes** ☎ **02 35 07 18 00**

La City
Fashionable clothes for affluent shoppers, displayed in a fine corner building with splendid carved window frames.
✉ **78 rue du Gros-Horloge** ☎ **02 35 07 51 11**

Florence Kooijman
A shoe designer who also has outlets in Lille, le Touquet and Amiens. Elegant shoes and ankle boots in suede or leather at reasonable prices.
✉ **11 rue Ganterie** ☎ **02 35 89 35 81**

The Northeast

Honfleur
La Payse
Ethnic jewellery and bags, woolly jumpers and scarves, and miscellaneous gifts.
✉ **rue du Dauphin**

Caen

Maison du Pantalon
Trousers and jeans for men and women, plus shirts, gloves, ties and accessories.
✉ **35 rue St-Pierre** ☎ **02 31 86 09 17**

Central Normandy

Alençon
Boutique Virginie
Examples of different types of lace, including *point d'Alençon*, and a wide selection of other fabrics.
✉ **146 Grande Rue** ☎ **02 33 26 53 71**

Bayeux
Jean-Paul
Designer shirts, jackets, trousers, ties and coats for men, including Lacoste, Viaggio and Ted Lapidus.
✉ **rue St-Jean** ☎ **02 31 92 04 05**

Trouville
Au Loup de Mer
Fishermen's jumpers and waterproofs for the diehard sailor.
✉ **boulevard Fernand-Moureaux** ☎ **02 31 88 01 30**

Troc-Chic
Vintage clothes and hats dating from the 1940s to the 1960s.
✉ **80 rue des Bains** ☎ **02 31 81 09 19**

The Northwest

Cherbourg
Gulliver
Smart leather shoes for men and children, including a range of multicoloured suede shoes.
✉ **rue des Fosses** ☎ **02 33 53 83 83**

Studio Mod
Costume jewellery for stylish women.
✉ **rue au Blé** ☎ **02 33 94 06 04**

Food

Rouen

Héloin Anne-Marie
Delicious sweets, chocolates and other goodies such as *pains d'épices* (gingerbread), jams, marmalades and honey, all beautifully presented.
✉ **98 rue des Carmes** ☎ **02 35 71 02 94**

Pierrette-Lamy
A small and very pretty *chocolaterie* with gift-wrapped goodies and individual treats.
✉ **rue St-Nicolas** ☎ **02 35 70 53 02**

The Northeast

Honfleur
Gribouille
Local products, including calvados, *poiré* and cider, jams, honey, olives, vinegar, cherries in calvados – all beautifully presented in an old grey-slate building with a double windowfront.
✉ **16 rue de l'Homme-de-Bois** ☎ **02 31 89 29 54**

La Petite Chine
Fresh pastries, *pains d'épices*, calvados, chocolates and a small tearoom behind the shop.
✉ **Corner of rue du Dauphin and rue de la Foulerie** ☎ **02 31 89 36 52**

Caen

Bon Appétit
Smart *charcuterie* selling tasty snacks – onion or fish tarts, egg and salmon jellies – and a range of meat products.
✉ **rue St-Pierre**

Hotot le Drakkar
A *chocolatier* with its own special creations and delicious calvados liqueurs, among other temptations.
✉ **rue St-Pierre** ☎ **02 32 41 28 00**

Roland
Pâtisserie with wonderful cakes and a few tables in the *salon de thé*.
✉ **rue St-Pierre** ☎ **02 31 86 24 53**

Central Normandy

Évreux
Charcuterie St-Antoine
Fine wines, cheeses, vegetable and fish pâtés, and exquisitely prepared fresh pastries and snacks. A mouth-watering browse.
✉ **rue Chartraine**

Vimoutiers
Musée du Camembert
A statue of Marie Harel, the discoverer of Camembert cheese, contemplates the plain square of this town in the cider-producing region of the Pays d'Auge. Vimoutiers was largely rebuilt after World War II and its chief interest for visitors is the museum in the tourist office, dedicated to the much-copied but rarely bettered (even within France) local soft cheese. Its history dates from the late 17th century though the cheese's fame is owed to Marie who came from the nearby village of Camembert. During the French Revolution she provided refuge to a priest who in return gave her a secret recipe for improving her own cheese making. The cheese is recognisable for its creamy interior and white crust – a perfect meal with just bread and cider.
✉ **10 avenue du Général de Gaulle** ☎ **02 33 39 30 29**

Fresh from the Farm
It's worth looking beyond the high street for many of the traditional Norman goods. Factories and farm shops are often the best places to sample and buy cheese, cider, honey, calvados, vegetables, fruit, and even durable products such as pottery and wool. For details contact the Comité Régional de Tourisme de Normandie (► 103).

Children's Attractions

Four-legged Friends
Horse-mad children will be in their element in Normandy, one of the foremost breeding centres in the country. The dappled Percheron horses, once bred to pull drays and buses, are still a famous feature of the Perche region; legend has it that their forebears were cobs and Arabs during the time of the crusades. At le Pin-au-Haras (➤ 70), a parade of beautiful horses pulling four-in-hand carriages jingles and trots through the grounds every Thursday at 3 (summer only). A demonstration of American cowboy riding techniques is the star turn at Quarter Horse Dream, at le Vitou, Vimoutiers, open daily (☎ 02 33 39 12 05).

Leisure and Amusement Parks

The Northeast

Clères
Parc du Bocasse
A family park with 80 games and rides, an enchanted river, pedalos, and its very own 'Niagara Falls'.
✉ Southwest of Clères, on D6 ☎ 02 35 33 22 25 🕐 Mid-Mar to Easter, Sep to mid-Oct, Wed and Sat 1–6, Sun and public hols 10–7; Easter hol–early Sep, daily 10–6 ✋ Expensive

Gisors
Parc de Loisirs du Bois d'Hérouval
A hundred or so games and activities especially designed for children, just beyond the Normandy border.
✉ 1km south of Gisors, off D915 ☎ 02 32 55 33 76 🕐 Easter–late Sep, daily 10–7 ✋ Moderate

Le Havre
Le Canyon
Fifty rides and games include Wild West fun and water slides.
✉ Epretot, 15km northeast of Le Havre, off N15 ☎ 02 35 20 42 69 🕐 Jun–Aug, daily 10:30–7; Mar–May, Sep to mid-Nov, Wed and weekend ✋ Moderate

Caen
Festyland
Plenty of choice for the energetic: bouncy castles, water rides and slides, go-karts, and toboggans.
✉ Bretteville-sur-Odon, outskirts of Caen ☎ 02 31 75 04 04 🕐 First Sun in Apr–last Sun in Sep, daily 11–7 ✋ Expensive

Central Normandy

Thury-Harcourt
Le Traspy
Aquatic centre with pool, water chutes, toboggans and other activities involving a good soaking.
✉ Signed in Thury-Harcourt ☎ 02 31 79 03 18 🕐 School hols Mon–Fri 10–12, 2:30–5, Sat 2:30–4 ✋ Moderate

The Northwest

Mortain
Parc de Loisirs L'Ange Michel
Laid out over 10ha near the Lac de Vezins. Giant (50m) toboggan, pony rides, children's electric cars and a mini-train.
✉ St-Martin-de-Landelles, south of St-Hilaire-du-Harcouët, on D977 west of Mortain ☎ 02 33 49 04 74 🕐 Jun–Aug, daily from 11; Apr, May, Sep, weekend and public hols from 1:30 ✋ Moderate

Model and Tourist Trains

Central Normandy

Clécy
Musée du Chemin de Fer Miniature
Claimed to be one of the largest model railways in Europe. Little locomotives – 220 of them – thunder along 430m of track around a scaled-down version of the Suisse Normande. A slightly larger train carries children round the grounds.
✉ D562, 38km southwest of Caen ☎ 02 31 69 07 13 🕐 Easter–end Sep, daily 10–12, 2:15–6; in low season, Sun 2–5. Closed 15 Dec–1 Mar ✋ Moderate

The Northwest

Mortain
Le Village Enchanté
A model train travels around this fairyland village which has the added attractions of crafts, a park and a puppet theatre.

✉ Bellefontaine, 6km north of Mortain, on D33 ☎ 02 33 59 01 93 ◉ Easter–end Sep, daily 10–7 🖐 Moderate

St-Lô
Mini-Train des Marais
Red-capped drivers operate the 'marshland mini-train', pulling child-size wagons around a 20cm-gauge track.

✉ Marchésieux, 6km east of Periers, on D900 west of St-Lô ☎ 02 33 05 15 54 ◉ Jul–end Aug, daily 2:30–dusk; Apr–Oct, weekend only 🖐 Cheap

Zoos and Aquariums

Central Normandy

Courseulles-sur-Mer
La Maison de la Mer
A journey through the sea tunnel leads to views of undersea life; the shell collection is worth visiting.

✉ place du 6 Juin ☎ 02 31 37 92 58 ◉ May, Jun, Sep, daily 9–1, 2–7; Jul, Aug, 9–7; Oct–end Apr, Tue–Sun 10–12, 2–6 🖐 Moderate

Thury-Harcourt
Parc Zoologique de la Cabosse
Giraffes and other wild animals wander through 10ha of wooded parkland. Area for picnics.

✉ Jurques, 20km west, between Caen and Vire ☎ 02 31 77 80 58 ◉ Mid-Jan to end Mar, Oct, Nov, daily 1:30–5:30; Apr–end Sep, 10–6 🖐 Expensive

Trouville
Aquarium Écologique
No fewer than 60 tanks with tropical and local fish, and several varieties of shark. Also creepy-crawlies and reptiles, including Big Hug, a 6m python.

✉ Trouville beach ☎ 02 31 88 46 04 ◉ Easter–Jun, Sep, Oct, daily 10–12, 2–7; Jul, Aug, 10–7:30, Nov–Easter, 2–6:30 🖐 Moderate

The Northwest

Granville
L'Aquarium du Roc
Fish, shells and models; same opening times and charges as the nearby Féerie des Coquillages (shell palace and light show), and the Palais Minéral et Jardin des Papillons (minerals, butterflies).

✉ boulevarde Vaufleury ☎ 02 33 50 19 83 ◉ Daily 9–7:30

Le Mont-St-Michel
Reptilarium du Mont-St-Michel
As well as the appeal of crocodiles and iguanas, pythons and boas, children can explore tunnels, ladders, a suspension bridge, pyramids, towers and a maze. The reptilarium is situated at Beauvoir, on the mainland opposite the mount.

✉ 62 route du Mont-St-Michel ☎ 02 33 68 11 18 ◉ Apr–end Sep, daily 10–7; Oct–Mar, 2–6. Closed weekends Jan 🖐 Moderate

Villedieu-les-Poëles
Parc Zoologique Champrepus
A 6ha floral park provides the pleasant setting for a 2km route that offers sightings of around 90 different animal species. An added attraction here is a small amusement park.

✉ Champrepus, 8km west of Villedieu-les-Poëles ☎ 02 33 61 30 74 ◉ Early Feb to end Mar, daily 1:30–6; Apr–Sep, 10–7. Closed mid-Nov to early Feb 🖐 Expensive

Tourist Trains
Children can ride through several Norman resorts in open wagons pulled at a sedate pace by mini-locomotives. Services leave daily from: the promenade Marcel Proust in Cabourg (July and August); the tourist office, place St-Pierre, in Caen; the town hall in Deauville; the harbour car park in Honfleur; the car park (La Basilique) in Lisieux; the beach at Trouville (daily July and August, weekends all year), and from the Town Hall in Viller-sur-Mer (July and August).

Music and Theatre

Church Music

Keep an eye out for free or inexpensive concerts held at churches and cathedrals all over the region, with a particularly good choice in Rouen and Le Havre. These may include organ recitals, chamber groups or choral works; some of the smaller concerts take place at lunchtime. Events are usually publicised on the church noticeboards and at the local tourist office, and included on the listings page of the regional newspaper, *Paris-Normandie*.

Theatres and Concert Halls

Rouen

Opera de Rouen

Major operatic and ballet productions, plus classical concerts, staged in a modern building overlooking the Seine.

✉ **quai de la Bourse** ☎ **02 35 71 41 36**

Théâtre des Deux Rives

Classical drama: repertoire includes Shakespeare, Gorky and the French greats.

✉ **48 rue Louis Ricard** ☎ **02 35 70 22 82**

Théâtre Duchamp-Villon

A theatre space in the modern Centre St-Sever, in the southern suburbs. Productions include a season of modern ballet works.

✉ **16 place de la Verrière, Centre St-Sever** ☎ **02 35 18 28 10** 🚇 **St-Sever** 🚌 **7, 12, 33**

Théâtre Maxime Gorki

Musical productions of modern and traditional European works, including cabaret evenings and jazz concerts.

✉ **rue François Mitterand, Petit Quévilly** ☎ **02 35 03 29 78**

The Northeast

Le Havre

Théâtre des Bains Douches

An interesting range of contemporary and experimental drama productions, as well as some fringe music events.

✉ **22 rue Louis Lobasso** ☎ **02 35 47 63 09**

Théâtre de l'Hôtel de Ville

Popular productions and family shows in an annexe of the city's modern town hall, overlooking the central square's lawns and fountains.

✉ **place de l'Hôtel de Ville** ☎ **02 35 19 45 74**

Le Volcan

Dance, theatre and music form an adventurous programme of classical and modern work. Also changing exhibitions of photography and talks.

✉ **Espace Oscar Niemeyer** ☎ **02 35 19 10 10**

Caen

Théâtre de Caen

Contemporary and traditional productions of music, opera, drama and dance.

✉ **135 Boulevard du Maréchal Leclerc** ☎ **02 31 30 48 20**

Central Normandy

Évreux

La Théâtre d'Évreux – Scène Nationale

A lively programme of events including seasons of films in conjunction with the Cinéma Victor Hugo, plus a varied range of dance, music and drama productions.

✉ **place du Général de Gaulle** ☎ **02 32 78 85 25**

Lisieux

Théâtre de Lisieux

Interesting touring productions, including contemporary drama, at a very traditional venue.

✉ **2 rue au Char** ☎ **02 31 61 04 40**

The Northwest

Cherbourg

Théâtre de Cherbourg

Set in a spectacularly ornate

building with a good café-restaurant attached; visiting orchestras, dance troupes and drama companies are included in a lively programme.

✉ place Général-de-Gaulle
☎ 02 33 88 55 55

Coutances
Théâtre Municipal de Coutances
The varied programme includes classical and popular music, traditional and new drama, dance and comedy.

✉ Rue Milon ☎ 02 33 76 78 50

Live Music Venues

Rouen

Le Bateau Ivre
Cabaret acts and a variety of musical events at an informal venue.

✉ 17 rue des Sapins ☎ 02 35 70 09 05 🕐 Tue–Wed till 2AM, Thu–Sat till 4AM

La Bertelière
A piano bar on the eastern outskirts of Rouen, near the railway line.

✉ 164 le Mesnic Gremichon, St-Martin-du-Vivier ☎ 02 35 60 44 00 🕐 Closed Sat lunch, Sun eve

Le Boston
The upmarket piano bar of the Hôtel Mercure Champ de Mars, on the road heading east out of the city.

✉ avenue Aristide Briand
☎ 02 35 52 42 32

Le Dieppe
Another hotel piano bar, in the Hôtel de Dieppe opposite the railway station.

✉ place Bernard Tissot ☎ 02 35 71 96 00

Le Nickel Chrome
Jazz, rock and blues performed by live bands from 11PM.

✉ 26 rue St-Étienne-des-Tonneliers ☎ 02 35 15 37 37

🕐 Tue–Thu until 2AM, Fri, Sat until 4AM

The Northeast

Le Havre
Brazil Café
A cocktail bar and café with occasional jazz evenings; near the Espace Oscar Niemeyer.

✉ 78 rue Voltaire ☎ 02 35 21 02 21

Greenish Pub
Rock bands sometimes perform at this lively pub which has a regular happy hour (8 till 9).

✉ 35 rue Lemaistre ☎ 02 35 22 89 33

L'Hermès
Punk rock lives on in this bar, where retro gigs are staged for a token entrance fee.

✉ 348 rue Aristide Briand
☎ 02 35 24 35 84

McDaid's
An Irish theme pub that sells Guinness, has a pool table, and features folk, rock and jazz bands on Thursdays and Fridays.

✉ 97 rue Paul Doumer ☎ 02 35 41 30 40 🕐 2PM–2AM

Caen

Au Big Band Café
Rock, blues and jazz performed live every Tuesday night.

✉ av du Haut Crépon, Hérouville ☎ 02 31 47 96 13

Texas Coyote
American-style bar with US rock music.

✉ 44 rue de Bras ☎ 02 31 38 83 13

The Northwest

Cherbourg
Casino Cherbourg
Disco, pub and restaurant on the quayside.

✉ quai Alexandre III ☎ 02 33 20 53 35

Cinemas
There's little problem finding mainstream movies, especially in Normandy's larger centres. Rouen has the multiscreen Gaumont (28 rue de la République) and UGC Les Clubs (75 rue de Général Leclerc), plus a cinema in the Centre St-Sever, across the river, and vintage and fringe films at Ariel (place Colbert) and Melville (12 rue St-Etienne). Le Havre has a choice including Eden, in the Espace Oscar Niemeyer, and there are several in Caen, including the Cinéma de Paris (12 avenue du 6 Juin), and Cinéma Lux (avenue Ste-Thérèse). Films marked 'VO' (*Version Originale*) are usually British or American, with the original soundtracks and French subtitles (*soustitres*).

Sport

Sport of Kings
Horse racing and horse breeding are big business in Normandy. Deauville's thoroughbred racehorse market turns over 150 million francs a year, and there are racecourses all over the region. Two organisations can provide details of courses and fixtures (which take place all through the year): the Fédération Régionale des Sociétés de Courses, BP 43, 14502 Vire (☎ 02 31 68 09 04); and the Ligue de Normandie des Sports Équestres, 10 place Demi-Lune, 14000 Caen (☎ 02 31 84 61 87).

Fishing and Watersports
There is plenty of opportunity for fishing in rivers, lakes and the sea (from pier or boat). Other popular sports are sailing, canoeing, kayaking, sand yachting or windsurfing. For information on clubs and organisations, contact the tourist office for each *département* (➤ 120). For details of sailing schools and yachting clubs, contact:

Centre Régional de Nautisme
✉ boulevard des Amiraux, Port de Hérel, 50400 Granville ☎ 02 33 91 22 60

Balleroy
Parc de Loisirs Cahagnolles
Leisure park has a 1.5ha lake for fishing, also tennis and a campsite.
✉ Cahagnolles, 6km east of Balleroy ☎ 02 31 21 63 59

Dives-sur-Mer
Sea-fishing trips on a fully equipped 12m boat, the *Pourquoi Pas*, all year.
☎ 02 31 24 46 15 (reservations)

Brionne
Parc de Loisirs
Summer sailing, fishing and swimming in a centre open all year. A sailing school offers lessons between June and October.
☎ 02 32 43 66 11

Lisieux
Les Étangs de Fierville
Trout, pike, carp, perch and more on full- or half-day fishing outings at a series of lakes.
✉ Fierville les Parcs, between Lisieux and Pont-l'Évêque ☎ 02 31 64 98 20

Rouen
Espace Régional Léry-Poses
Activities include water-skiing, windsurfing, kayaking, swimming, sailing, rowing and fishing at an open-air leisure centre covering over 1,500ha in a bend of the Seine. Access to two lakes: le Lac des Deux Amants and le Lac du Mesnil.
✉ Léry-Poses, south of Rouen, on D110 ☎ 02 32 59 13 13

Golf
The Golfing Passport is a scheme operated in Calvados that allows use of five green fees on five different courses (from a selection of six) on nine consecutive days. It must be booked in advance, though no payment is due until you arrive at the first golf course. Obtain the passport from:

Calvados Tourisme
✉ place du Canada, 14000 Caen ☎ 02 31 27 90 30

Caen
Golf de Caen 'Le Vallon'
A 27-hole course with a putting green, practice course, restaurant and clubhouse.
✉ 14112 Biéville-Beuville, 8km north of Caen ☎ 02 31 94 72 09

Cherbourg
La Glacerie
Six indoor and 12 outdoor practice greens, plus a 9-hole course. Golf practice schools Wednesday and Saturday.
✉ Domaines des Roches, La Glacerie, 4km southeast of Cherbourg, on D122 ☎ 02 33 44 45 48

Clécy
Golf de Clécy-Cantelou
Eighteen holes on the manor

green, plus a putting green, clubhouse and restaurant.

✉ **Manoir de Cantelou, 30km south of Caen on D562** ☎ 02 31 69 72 72

Deauville
New Golf de Deauville
Open daily (except Tuesday in winter), this 27-hole course also has a training green, golf shop and restaurant.

✉ **2km south of Deauville, off D278** ☎ 02 31 14 24 24

Dieppe
Golf de Dieppe
Established in 1897, this is one of Normandy's oldest golf courses; 18 holes.

✉ **Western outskirts of Dieppe, off D75** ☎ 02 35 84 25 05

Golf de Garcelles
Two 9-hole courses, with a training bunker and putting green.

✉ **route de Falaise, Garcelles-Secqueville, 6km south of Caen** ☎ 02 31 39 09 09

Granville
Golf de Granville
27 holes along the seafront, a covered practice course, and two putting greens.

✉ **3km north of Granville at Bréville-sur-Mer, on D236/GR 223** ☎ 02 33 50 23 06

Le Havre
Golf du Havre
An 18-hole course where golfers have been swinging since the 1930s.

✉ **Octeville-sur-Mer, 10km north of Le Havre** ☎ 02 35 46 36 50

Rouen
Golf de Rouen
The city's 18-hole golf club, founded in 1911.

✉ **Mont-St-Aignon, 5km north of Rouen on D43** ☎ 02 35 76 38 65

Equestrian Tourism
The 'land of the horse' is very well geared to horse-related

holidays, and several clubs and centres offer tours on horseback, or visits to stud farms. Information on these, and on riding schools and pony clubs, is available from:

Association Régionale de Tourisme Équestre
✉ **La Maillardière 50480 Ste-Marie-du-Mont** ☎ 02 33 71 58 23

Comité Ornais de Tourisme Équestre, de Randonnée et d'Équitation de Loisirs
☎ 02 33 29 19 92 or 02 33 35 31 75

Comité Départemental de Tourisme Équestre du Calvados
✉ **Randonnée 14, place du Canada, Caen** ☎ 02 31 85 52 72

Comité Départemental de Tourisme Équestre et Gîte de France de la Manche
✉ **rue Howard Houston, Canisy** ☎ 02 33 56 76 84

Cycling
Cycles can be hired at several railway stations through the region and can be taken free of charge on some train services. The *département* tourist offices provide lists of cycle hire centres. Information on cycling and route maps can be obtained from:

Fédération Française de Cyclotourisme (Ligue Basse-Normandie)
✉ **20 rue du Beau-Site, 14250 Tilly/Seulles** ☎ 02 31 80 50 33

Fédération Française de Cyclotourisme (Ligue Haute-Normandie)
✉ **21 rue de l'Enseigne-Renaud, 76000 Rouen** ☎ 02 35 89 45 06

Fédération Française de Cyclotourisme
✉ **8 rue Jean-Marie-Jégo, 75013 Paris** ☎ 01 44 16 88 88

Hiking and Walking
The Institut Géographique National (IGN) publishes large-scale maps showing long-distance paths (marked as GR, or Grandes Randonnés), several of which cross parts of Normandy. Guides that list paths are available from the Fédération Française de la Randonnée Pédestre, 64 rue de Gergovie, 75014 Paris (☎ 01 45 45 31 02); and, within Normandy, the Comité Départemental de Randonnée Pédestre de l'Orne, 2 rue René Fonck, 61000 Alençon (☎ 02 33 29 33 74); the Comité Départemental de Tourisme Pédestre du Calvados, 6 promenade de Madame-de-Sévigné, 14050 Caen (☎ 02 31 89 39 07); and the Comité Départemental de la Randonnée Pédestre de la Manche, Maison du Département, 50008 St-Lô (☎ 02 33 05 98 70).

What's On When

Festive France
A booklet called *Festive France* lists precise dates and venues (where possible) for festivals, sound-and-light performances, shows, and other events in France, including Normandy. It is published each year by Maison de la France, 8 avenue de l'Opéra, 75001 Paris, France (☎ 01 42 96 10 23). It also gives telephone and fax numbers for the organisers of each event. Alternatively, contact the local tourist office for each *département* (➤ 120).

January–April
Apple markets, Parc Naturel Régional de Brotonne (ask at tourist offices for venues).

March
Tree Fair, Lisieux (first week).
Fair celebrating Mortagne-au-Perche's traditional blood-sausage (first week).
Scandinavian Film Festival, Rouen.

April
Rouen International Fair (first two weeks).

April–May
Street Theatre Festival, Fécamp.

May
Jazz under the Apple Trees, Coutances.
Geranium Fair, Beuvron-en-Auge.
Spring Fair (religious and folk events), le Mont-St-Michel.
Seafarers' Pilgrimage, Honfleur.
Jeanne d'Arc Festival, Rouen.

June
Music Festival, venues throughout Orne.
Blessing of the Sea and Sea Festival, Le Havre.
Anniversary of Normandy Landings, D-Day Beaches (6 June).
Folklore Festival, Trouville.

June–October
Eure Summer Festival, venues throughout Eure.

July
Medieval Festival, Bayeux.
Pilgrimage across the beaches, le Mont-St-Michel.
Puppet Festival, Dives-sur-Mer.

July–August
Coutances Summer Festival.

August
Thoroughbred Yearling Auction and Polo Lancel Cup, Deauville.
Turkey Market, Lisieux.
Ancient Music Festival, Dieppe.
Cheese Fair, Livarot.
Les Traversées de Tatihou (traditional music and dancing), Île de Tatihou.

August–September
Presentation of stallions and horse teams of the national stud, St-Lô.

September
Sea Festival (La Mer en Fête), Le Havre.
Horse racing, parade and presentation of studs, le Pin-au-Haras.
Caen International Fair.
American Film Festival, Deauville.
Ancient Ste-Croix Fair, Lessay.
International Mushroom Fair, Bellême.
Music Festival, Orne.

October
Horse Week, locations throughout Calvados.
Cider Market and Festival, Beuvron-en-Auge.
Shrimp Festival, Honfleur.
International Flower Show, Lisieux.
Jacques Vabre Transatlantic Race, Le Havre.
Antique Fair, Rouen.

November
Horse jumping (Jump'Orne), Alençon.
Apple Festival, Le Havre.

December
Turkey Fair, Sées.

Practical Matters

Above: *the best way to travel in rural Normandy*
Right: *a sign of accommodation with character*

TIME DIFFERENCES

GMT	France	Germany	USA (NY)	Netherlands	Spain
12 noon	1PM	1PM	7AM	1PM	1PM

BEFORE YOU GO

WHAT YOU NEED

- ● Required
- ○ Suggested
- ▲ Not required

	UK	Germany	USA	Netherlands	Spain
Passport/National Identity Card	●	●	●	●	●
Visa	▲	▲	▲	▲	▲
Onward or Return Ticket	▲	▲	▲	▲	▲
Health Inoculations (tetanus and polio)	▲	▲	▲	▲	▲
Health Documentation (reciprocal agreement document, ➤ 123, Health)	●	●	●	●	●
Travel Insurance	○	○	○	○	○
Driving Licence (national)	●	●	●	●	●
Car Insurance Certificate (if own car)	○	○	○	○	○
Car Registration Document (if own car)	●	●	●	●	●

WHEN TO GO

Caen

High season

Low season

7°C	8°C	12°C	13°C	17°C	20°C	22°C	22°C	20°C	15°C	11°C	8°C
JAN	FEB	MAR	APR	MAY	JUN	JUL	AUG	SEP	OCT	NOV	DEC

Very wet Wet Cloud Sun Showers

TOURIST OFFICES

In the UK
French Tourist Office
178 Piccadilly
London W1V OAL
☎ 020 7399 3500
(recorded information)
fax 020 493 6594

Normandy Tourist Board
The Old Bakery
Bath Hill
Keynsham
Bristol BS18 1HG
☎ 0117 986 0386
fax 0117 986 0379

In the USA
French Government
Tourist Office
444 Madison Avenue
16th floor
New York NY 10022
☎ 212/838 7800
fax 212/838 7855

POLICE 17

FIRE 18

AMBULANCE 15

SOS TRAVELLERS 04 91 62 12 80

WHEN YOU ARE THERE

ARRIVING

Airports at Caen, Cherbourg, Deauville, Le Havre and Rouen take international flights. Ferries travel from the UK to Cherbourg, Ouistreham, Le Havre and Dieppe, and from Ireland to Cherbourg and Le Havre. Several centres are served by fast trains from Paris. The junction of the A28 and A16 roads at Abbeville provides a direct link between Normandy and the Eurotunnel at Calais.

Rouen Airport	Journey Times	
Kilometres to city centre	🚇	N/A
	🚌	N/A
7 kilometres	🚗	10 minutes

MONEY

In January 2002 euro banknotes and coins will come into circulation with a value of 6.55 French francs to 1 euro and for a short time a dual pricing system will operate. On 28 February 2002 French francs will be withdrawn from use.

Euro notes will be issued in denominations of 5, 10, 20, 50, 100, 200 and 500 euros. Coins will be issued in denominations of 1 and 2 euros and 1, 2, 5, 20 and 50 cents; 100 cents = €1.

Travellers' cheques and cash can be changed at most banks. Visa, Access and MasterCard are generally accepted in hotels and restaurants.

TIME

France is one hour ahead of Greenwich Mean Time (GMT+1), but from late March, when clocks are put forward one hour, until late October French summer time (GMT+2) operates.

CUSTOMS

YES

Goods Obtained Duty Free Inside the EU or Goods Bought Outside the EU (Limits):
Alcohol over 22% vol: 1L or
Alcohol not over 22% vol: 2L
Still table wine: 2L
Cigarettes: 200 or
Cigars: 50 or
Tobacco: 250g
Perfume: 60ml
Toilet water: 250ml
Goods Bought Duty and Tax Paid Inside the EU (Guidance Levels):
Alcohol over 22% vol: 10L
Alcohol not over 22% vol: 20L
Wine: 90L (max 60L sparkling)
Beer: 110L
Cigarettes: 800 or
Cigars: 200 or
Tobacco: 1kg
Perfume: no limit
Toilet water: no limit
You must be 17 or over to benefit from the alcohol and tobacco allowances.

NO

Drugs, firearms, ammunition, offensive weapons, obscene material, unlicensed animals.

119

UK
01 42 66 91 42
(Paris Embassy)
01 42 66 38 10
(Paris consulate)

Germany
01 42 99 78 00
(Paris Embassy)

USA
01 43 12 22 22
(Paris Embassy)

Netherlands
01 40 62 33 00
(Paris Embassy)

Spain
01 44 43 18 18
(Paris Embassy)
01 47 66 03 32
(Paris Consulate)

WHEN YOU ARE THERE

TOURIST OFFICES

Comité Régional du Tourisme de Normandie
● 14 rue Charles Corbeau
27000 Évreux
☎ 02 32 33 79 00

Departmental Tourist Offices
● Comité Départemental de Tourisme du Calvados
place du Canada
14000 Caen
☎ 02 31 27 90 30

● Comité Départemental de Tourisme de l'Eure
boulevard Georges-Chauvin
BP 367
27003 Évreux
☎ 02 32 62 04 27

● Comité Départemental de Tourisme d'Eure-et-Loir
10 rue du Dr Maunoury
BP 67
28002 Chartres cedex
☎ 02 37 84 01 00

● Comité Départemental de Tourisme de la Manche
route de Villedieu
50008 St-Lô
☎ 02 33 05 98 70

● Comité Départemental de Tourisme de l'Orne
88 rue St-Blaise
BP 50
61002 Alençon
☎ 02 33 28 88 71

● Comité Départemental de Tourisme de Seine-Maritime
6 rue Couronné
BP 60
76420 Bihorel-les-Rouen
☎ 02 35 12 10 18

NATIONAL HOLIDAYS

J	F	M	A	M	J	J	A	S	O	N	D
1		(2)	(2)	3(2)	(2)	1	1			2	1

1 Jan	New Year's Day
Mar/Apr	Easter Sunday and Monday
1 May	Labour Day
8 May	VE Day
May	Ascension Day
May/Jun	Whit Sunday and Monday
14 Jul	Bastille Day
15 Aug	Assumption Day
1 Nov	All Saints' Day
11 Nov	Remembrance Day
25 Dec	Christmas Day

OPENING HOURS

○ Shops	● Post Offices
● Offices	◐ Museums/Monuments
◐ Banks	◐ Pharmacies

8AM 9AM 10AM NOON 1PM 2PM 4PM 5PM 7PM

□ Day	□ Midday
□ Evening	

In addition to the times shown above, afternoon times of shops in summer can extend in the most popular centres. Most shops close Sunday and many on Monday. Small food shops open from 7AM and may open Sunday morning. Large department stores do not close for lunch and hypermarkets open 10AM to 9 or 10PM, but may shut Monday morning. Banks are closed Sunday as well as Saturday or Monday. Museums and monuments have extended summer hours. Many close one day a week: either Monday (municipal ones) or Tuesday (national ones).

DRIVE ON THE
RIGHT

TOILETS
FREE

★ ★
★ ★

PUBLIC TRANSPORT

 Internal Flights Air Atlantique operates daily flights from Paris (Roissy-Charles de Gaulle and Orly) to Cherbourg (just under an

 Trains Main lines connect Paris with Rouen, Le Havre, Dieppe, Caen, Cherbourg and Granville. Within Normandy there is a wide rail network linking all the main centres and many smaller towns. Free timetables are available from tourist offices for regional transport (train lines and inter-centre buses) in Haute-Normandie and Basse-Normandie.

 Buses Most sizeable towns have a bus station (*gare routière*). Some lines operate in conjunction with SNCF trains; other, local services link smaller towns and villages, and Bus verts du Calvados operate some of the longer rural lines. Apart from the regional transport lines (see Trains), timetables are quite difficult to find outside major centres such as Rouen and Caen, but times are often posted on the bus stops themselves.

 Boats and Ferries Émeraude Lines run ferries to Jersey, with connections to Guernsey and Sark from Granville (☎ 02 33 50 16 36) and Carteret (☎ 02 33 52 61 39). Boats go to the Îles Chausey from Granville and to the Île Tatihou from St-Vaast-la-Hougue.

 Urban Transport Urban bus routes operate in larger cities. Rouen has installed a Métrobus that links both banks of the Seine and extends south into the suburbs. A booklet giving details of the Métrobus is available free from the Rouen tourist office, 25 place de la Cathédrale (☎ 02

CAR RENTAL

 All large towns have car-rental agencies at their airports and railway stations. Car hire is expensive, but airlines and tour operators offer fly-drive and French Railways (SNCF) train-car packages, often more economical than hiring locally.

TAXIS

 Taxis are a costlier option than public transport. They pick up at taxi ranks (*stations de taxi*) found at railway stations and airports. Hotels and restaurants can usually give a taxi call number. Check the taxi has a meter; there is a pick-up charge plus a rate per minute.

DRIVING

 Speed limits on toll motorways (autoroutes): **130kph** (**110kph** when wet); non-toll motorways and dual carriageways: **110kph** (**100kph** when wet). In fog (visibility less than 50m): **50kph** all roads

 Speed limits on country roads: **90kph** (**80kph** when wet)

 Speed limits on urban roads: **50kph** (limit starts at town sign)

 Must be worn in front seats at all times and in rear seats where fitted.

 Random breath-testing is frequent. Limit: 0.05% alcohol per litre of blood.

 Petrol (*essence*) including unleaded (*sans plomb*), and diesel (*gasoil*) is widely available. Petrol stations are numerous along main roads but rarer in rural areas. Some on minor roads are closed on Sundays. Maps showing petrol stations are available

A red warning triangle must be carried if your car has no hazard warning lights. Place the triangle 30m behind the car in the event of an accident or breakdown. On motorways ring from emergency phones (every 2km) to contact the breakdown service. Off motorways, police will advise on local breakdown services.

PERSONAL SAFETY

The *Police Municipale* (blue uniforms) carry out police duties in cities and towns. The *Gendarmes* (blue trousers, black jackets, white belts), the national police force, cover the countryside and smaller places. The *CRS* deal with emergencies and also look after safety on beaches.

To avoid danger or theft:
• Do not use unmanned roadside rest areas at night.
• Cars, especially foreign cars, should be secured.
• In crowded places, beware of pickpockets.

Police assistance:
☎ **17**

from any call box

TELEPHONES

Telephone numbers in France comprise ten digits; the first two for Normandy numbers are 02 (omit 0 if dialling from the UK). Many public phones use pre-paid cards (*télécartes*); these can be bought at post offices, *bureaux de tabac* and branches of France Télécom. They come in units of 50 or 120.

International Dialling Codes	
From France:	
UK:	**00 44**
Germany:	**00 49**
USA & Canada:	**00 1**
Netherlands:	**00 31**
Spain:	**00 34**

POST

The PTT (*Postes et Télécommunications*) deals with mail and telephone services. Outside main centres, post offices open shorter hours and may close 12–2. Letter boxes are yellow. Open: 8AM–7PM (till 12 Sat). Closed: Sun. Main post office in Rouen: 45 rue Jeanne d'Arc (☎ 02 35 15 66 73).

ELECTRICITY

The French power supply is: 220 volts
Type of socket:

Round two-hole sockets taking two-round-pin (or occasionally three-round-pin) plugs. British visitors should bring an adaptor; US visitors a voltage transformer.

TIPS/GRATUITIES

Yes ✓ No ✗		
Restaurants (service incl., tip optional)	✗	
Cafés/Bar (service incl., tip optional)	✗	
Hotels (service incl., tip optional	✗	
Hairdressers	✓	€1
Taxis	✓	€1
Tour guides	✓	€1
Cinema usherettes	✓	€1
Cloakroom attendants	✓	change
Toilet attendants	✓	change

HEALTH

Insurance
Nationals of EU and certain other countries can get medical treatment in France at reduced cost on production of a qualifying form (Form E111 for Britons), although private medical insurance is still advised and is essential for all other visitors.

Dental Services
As for general medical treatment (see above, **Insurance**), nationals of EU countries can obtain dental treatment at reduced cost. About 70 per cent of a dentist's standard fee can be refunded. Private medical insurance is still advisable for all.

Sun Advice
The sunniest (and hottest) months are July and August, but the good weather can start in June and continue to October. Generally the weather is relatively mild, though take care on the beach and when walking. Drink plenty of fluids, wear a hat and make sure you apply a good sunscreen.

Drugs
Pharmacies – recognised by their green cross sign – have qualified staff able to offer medical advice, provide first aid, and prescribe and provide a wide range of drugs, though some are available by prescription (*ordonnance*) only.

Safe Water
It is safe to drink tap water served in hotels and restaurants, but never drink from a tap marked *eau non potable* (not drinking water). Many prefer the taste of bottled water, which is cheap and widely available.

CONCESSIONS

Students/Youths A youth card (*Carte Jeune*), available to those under 26, entitles holders to various discounts on public transport, museum admissions, entertainments, shopping and other facilities (including meals in university canteens): ask at tourist offices and post offices for details.

Senior Citizens A number of tour companies offer special arrangements for senior citizens; for further information contact the French Tourist Office (➤ 118, **Tourist Offices**). Senior citizens (aged over 60) are eligible for reduced or free entrance to sights, and (aged over 65) fare discounts on public transport.

CLOTHING SIZES

France	UK	Rest of Europe	USA		
46	36	46	36		
48	38	48	38		
50	40	50	40		Suits
52	42	52	42		
54	44	54	44		
56	46	56	46		
41	7	41	8		
42	7.5	42	8.5		
43	8.5	43	9.5		Shoes
44	9.5	44	10.5		
45	10.5	45	11.5		
46	11	46	12		
37	14.5	37	14.5		
38	15	38	15		
39/40	15.5	39/40	15.5		Shirts
41	16	41	16		
42	16.5	42	16.5		
43	17	43	17		
36	8	34	6		
38	10	36	8		
40	12	38	10		Dresses
42	14	40	12		
44	16	42	14		
46	18	44	16		
38	4.5	38	6		
38	5	38	6.5		
39	5.5	39	7		Shoes
39	6	39	7.5		
40	6.5	40	8		
41	7	41	8.5		

WHEN DEPARTING

- Remember to contact the airport on the day before leaving to ensure the flight details are unchanged.
- If travelling by ferry you must check in no later than the time specified on your ticket.
- Check the duty-free limits of the country you are entering before departure.

LANGUAGE

French is the native language. English is spoken widely, especially by those involved in the tourist trade and working in the larger and most popular centres; in smaller, rural places fewer people speak English. In any case, attempts to speak French, or at least to greet others in French, will be much appreciated. Below is a list of helpful words. More extensive coverage can be found in the AA's *Essential French Phrase Book*.

hotel	l'hôtel	rate	le tarif
guest house	chambre d'hôte	breakfast	le petit déjeuner
room	la chambre	toilet	les toilettes
single room	une personne	bathroom	la salle de bain
double room	deux personnes	shower	la douche
per person	par personne	balcony	le balcon
per room	par chambre	key	la clef/clé
one/two nights	une/deux nuits	chambermaid	femme
reservation	la réservation		de chambre

bank	la banque	banknote	le billet
exchange office	le bureau de	coin	la pièce
	change	credit card	la carte de crédit
post office	la poste		le chèque de
cashier	le caissier	travellers'	voyage
foreign	le change	cheque	le taux de
exchange	extérieur	exchange rate	change
English pound	la livre sterling		

restaurant	la restaurant	starter	le hors d'œuvre
café	le café	main course	le plat principal
table	la table	dish of the day	le plat du jour
menu	le menu	dessert	le dessert
set menu	le menu du jour	drink	la boisson
wine list	la carte des vins	waiter	le garçon
lunch	le déjeuner	waitress	la serveuse
dinner	le dîner	the bill	l'addition

aeroplane	l'avion	single/return	simple/retour
airport	l'aéroport	ticket office	le guichet
train	le train	timetable	l'horaire
train station	la gare	seat	la place
bus	l'autobus	first class	première classe
bus station	la gare routière	second class	seconde classe
ferry/boat	le bateau	non-smoking	non-fumeurs
port	le port	reserved	réservé
ticket	le billet	window	la fenêtre

yes	oui	today	aujourd'hui
no	non	tomorrow	demain
please	s'il vous plaît	yesterday	hier
thank you	merci	how much?	combien?
hello	bonjour	expensive	cher
goodbye	au revoir	open	ouvert
goodnight	bonsoir	closed	fermé
sorry	pardon	you're welcome	de rien
excuse me	excusez-moi	okay	d'accord
help!	au secours!	I don't know	je ne sais pas

INDEX

Acknowledgements

The Automobile Association would like to thank the following photographers and libraries for their assistance in the preparation of this book: BRIDGEMAN ART LIBRARY, LONDON 14b, Self Portrait, 1917 by Claude Monet (1840–1926) Musée D'Orsay, Paris, France/Bridgeman Art Gallery, London/New York, 22b Music at the Customs House at Le Havre by Raoul Dufy (1877–1953) Musée Des Beaux-Arts André Malraux, Le Havre/Giraudon/Bridgeman Art Library, London; ROBERT HARDING PICTURE LIBRARY 5b; HULTON GETTY 11b; PICTURES COLOUR LIBRARY 28/29; POWERSTOCK/ZEFA 24/25; SPECTRUM COLOUR LIBRARY 10b, 58, 63b

The remaining photographs are held in the Association's own library (AA PHOTO LIBRARY) and were taken by Rob Moore, with the exception of pages 117b, 122a by J Edmanson; 122b by Paul Kenward; 2, 122c by Tony Oliver; F/cover c (Gros Horloge), e (cemetery), f (Bayeux Cathedral), h (lady), i, 7b, 8c, 15a, 16a, 17a, 17b, 18a, 19a, 19b, 20a, 20b, 21a, 21b, 22a, 23a, 24a, 25a, 26a, 26b, 27b, 28a, 37, 40b, 43b, 46b, 48, 55b, 57b, 62, 65a, 68b, 72b, 75b, 81, 82, 83, 84, 86, 88, 117a by Clive Sawyer; 9c, 89 by Barrie Smith and F/cover (a) and B/cover (Mont St Michel) by Rick Strange.

Author's Acknowledgements

Nia Williams wishes to thank Tony Evans, Dr Neil Kenny, and Stephen Rodgers and Lucy Walker of the Normandy Tourist Board for all their help and advice.

Revision Management: Pam Stagg

Dear Essential Traveller

Your comments, opinions and recommendations are very important to us. So please help us to improve our travel guides by taking a few minutes to complete this simple questionnaire.

You do not need a stamp (unless posted outside the UK). If you do not want to cut this page from your guide, then photocopy it or write your answers on a plain sheet of paper.

Send to: **The Editor, AA World Travel Guides, FREEPOST SCE 4598, Basingstoke RG21 4GY.**

Your recommendations…

We always encourage readers' recommendations for restaurants, nightlife or shopping – if your recommendation is used in the next edition of the guide, we will send you a *FREE* **AA** *Essential* **Guide** of your choice. Please state below the establishment name, location and your reasons for recommending it.

_____

_____

_____

_____

Please send me **AA** *Essential* _____

(*see list of titles inside the front cover*)

About this guide…

Which title did you buy?

AA *Essential* _____

Where did you buy it? _____

When? m m / y y

Why did you choose an AA *Essential* Guide? _____

_____

_____

_____

_____

Did this guide meet your expectations?

Exceeded ☐ Met all ☐ Met most ☐ Fell below ☐

Please give your reasons _____

_____

_____

_____

continued on next page…

Were there any aspects of this guide that you particularly liked? _____

_____

_____

_____

Is there anything we could have done better? _____

_____

_____

_____

_____

About you...

Name (*Mr/Mrs/Ms*) _____

    Address _____

_____

_____ Postcode _____

    Daytime tel nos _____

Which age group are you in?

    Under 25 ☐ 25–34 ☐ 35–44 ☐ 45–54 ☐ 55–64 ☐ 65+ ☐

How many trips do you make a year?

    Less than one ☐ One ☐ Two ☐ Three or more ☐

Are you an AA member? Yes ☐ No ☐

About your trip...

When did you book? m m / y y   When did you travel? m m / y y

How long did you stay? _____

Was it for business or leisure? _____

Did you buy any other travel guides for your trip?

    If yes, which ones? _____

_____

Thank you for taking the time to complete this questionnaire. Please send it to us as soon as possible, and remember, you do not need a stamp (*unless posted outside the UK*).

Happy Holidays!